GARY CARTWRIGHT

WANTED MAN
THE STORY OF MUKHTAR ABLYAZOV

A Manual for Criminals
on How to Avoid Punishment in the EU

London
2019

Published in UK
for EU Today LTD
by Cambridge International Press, © 2019
e-mail: cip.publisher@gmail.com
www.cambridgeinternationalpress.com

WANTED MAN: THE STORY OF MUKHTAR ABLYAZOV
A Manual for Criminals on How to Avoid Punishment in the EU
by Gary Cartwright ©

English

Editor Stephen M. Bland
Designer Alexandra Rey
Cover image by Philippe Merle

British Library Catalogue in Publication Data
A catalogue record for this book is available from the British Library
Library of Congress in Publication Data
A catalogue record for this book has been requested

ISBN: 978-1-910886-95-3

CONTENTS

FOREWORD BY THE EDITOR

With the tenth anniversary of his flight from the authorities in his homeland of Kazakhstan fast approaching, the raft of transnational court cases involving fugitive embezzler Mukhtar Ablyazov show no sign of abating. In a global saga which stretches from an institutional aversion to tackling kleptocracy in the United Kingdom to United States President Donald Trump's shady business partners, the murky world of Mukhtar Ablyazov even led his family to make a pit stop in the Central African Republic to pick up diplomatic passports. Yet despite having judgements against him totalling $4.9 billion in the British courts alone, almost six years since he fled from the UK to avoid three concurrent 22-month sentences for contempt of court, Ablyazov remains a free man.

So who is this criminal mastermind, a man found to have committed 'fraud on an epic scale' in the UK and sentenced in absentia in his homeland of having ordered the assassination of his erstwhile business partner? A country boy turned kleptocrat, in certain quarters estimates as to the total amount embezzled by Ablyazov stand at almost $10 billion, yet from his villa in France, Ablyazov continues to bemoan his plight to be a simple case of 'political persecution.' This is an argument supported by parties such as the NGO, the Open Dialog Foundation, whose activities, a report from a conference held in the European Parliament in November 2017 found, are funded by companies 'flagged and sanctioned by the West.'

With webs of shell companies which straddle the globe threatening democracy at every turn, the story of master fraudster Mukhtar Ablyazov and his entourage is shrouded in deliberately and intricately constructed layers of obfuscation. In his book, Cartwright shines a light on the extraordinary antics of the fugitive kleptocrat and his retinue. Exhaustively researched, yet succinct and easily comprehensible, Wanted Man: The Story of Mukhtar Ablyazov lays bare the startling facts behind this opaque tale.

— Stephen M. Bland,
award-winning author and journalist

PROLOGUE

A murder committed to facilitate fraud and theft on a scale the world has rarely, if ever, seen. The perpetrators closely associated with top officials and illegally funded companies linked to shadowy operators at the heart of politics in the European Union, and those responsible seemingly able to escape justice at will. This isn't the plot of a novel by John Grisham or Ian Fleming, but a harsh reality involving billions of dollars of stolen funds, a story which began in the days following the fall of the Soviet Union and continues today, with its perpetrators apparently always a step ahead of justice. It is a saga of criminality that calls into question the basic concept of justice. Is it impartial and applicable to all without fear or favour, or is it something that can be bought and paid for? Are judicial systems partial to those with enough money or political influence that has itself been obtained at a price?

The story begins in the post-Soviet Republic of Kazakhstan, a fledgling nation, but one with a proud people of Turkic and Mongol origins whose history stretches back over millennia. In this nation that has rapidly evolved from a vassal state to an emerging economy, a remarkable figure emerged. A young man from a humble background, Mukhtar Ablyazov quickly rose to the rank of minister in the government of the highly regarded President Nursultan Nazarbayev.

The dissolution of the Soviet Union in 1991 was widely unpredicted, with the West apparently unprepared. In hindsight, the end of the

Soviet Union following the dramatic collapse of the Berlin Wall in 1989 was inevitable. As the Union of Soviet Socialist Republics (USSR) experienced its final days, the Supreme Soviet left the constituent republics to fend for themselves. The Kremlin withdrew into survival mode and, under the guidance of President Boris Yeltsin, explored new avenues on how to protect Russia, historically the colonial master, including a brief flirtation with liberal democracy.

Whilst the West embraced the new situation and opened doors at every level to the former Soviet states, in the fledgling republics long-held animosities were to express themselves in a number of ways. In the former Yugoslavia, vicious warfare broke out with battle lines drawn along ethnic and religious grounds. Europe was again to witness heartrending scenes of citizens imprisoned behind barbed wire and subjected to starvation and brutality based simply on ethnicity and religion. Ethnic cleansing reappeared on the continent which had already given the world the words 'Holodomor' and 'Holocaust' just decades earlier and then naively told itself, 'never again.'

In the Baltic States, hatred of the former and much loathed Russian occupiers was expressed in the peaceful but to many provocative tearing down of Soviet-era monuments. In Ukraine, the desire for independence and self-determination that had long defined the country's relationship with its closest neighbour was reignited, and the seeds for the Orange Revolution of November 2004 were sown. All of this led down the long and painful road to the illegal annexation by Russia of Crimea in 2014 and the often covert Russian-backed military struggle in the Donbass that now pits Ukrainian against Ukrainian.

In Central Asia, a region often overlooked by the West, and indeed by the Kremlin itself, the seeds were quietly and carefully being sown for another revolution - a peaceful economic revolution. The republics of Kazakhstan, Kyrgyzstan, Tajikistan, Turkmenistan and Uzbekistan, along with their neighbour Azerbaijan were looking for their own places in the modern world. Each had its own traditions and values. Each had suffered in its own way under the Soviet yoke and each sought its own distinct path forward.

Kazakhstan demonstrated remarkably inspirational economic and social change, becoming the de facto leader of the region. Under the leadership of President Nursultan Nazarbayev, the vast but sparsely populated country was to rapidly embrace the difficult and sometimes tortuous transition from a controlled economy to a free market. This involved major changes in the country in terms of the introduction of appropriate legislation, of political and economic practices and in the mindset of the political elites and the people themselves.

The nation had been left scarred by failures in environmental policy associated with Soviet centralised planning. The Aral Sea, which had provided water, food and livelihoods for countless generations, was left a dried up wasteland by disastrous irrigation policies. Kazakhstan had also been used by the Soviet Union as a testing ground for nuclear weapons. The impact of this left a horrific impact on the environment and public health. There was much to be done.

The country has vast mineral resources, which include uranium and gold, and by carefully exploiting these riches in a sustainable manner and raising its international profile through positive and pro-active high-level engagement with international bodies, Kazakhstan has become the fastest growing and most stable economy in Central Asia. It is currently on track to achieve President Nazarbayev's stated aim of placing the country among the top thirty economies in the world.

Kazakhstan needed entrepreneurial leaders, and Mukhtar Ablyazov had such qualities. Often described as a 'financial genius,' a label that very few would disagree with, he was eventually to take control of one of Kazakhstan's largest financial institutions, BTA Bank. Whilst acting as chairman of the institution from 2005 to 2009, however, he was covertly building a criminal network through which he syphoned off astonishing sums of money, estimated to be between $6 to $7.6 billion, before fleeing the country.

The subject of an Interpol Red Notice and at least three extradition warrants, he was subsequently to fall afoul of a two-year sentence in England, which he escaped by slipping out of the country. Having languished in French custody since July 2013, on 9th, December 2016 Ablyazov was freed in an astonishing judicial about-face. In 2017, having been tried in absentia, he received a twenty-year sentence in his home country that has been unable to extradite him.

At the time of writing, Ablyazov is facing yet another trial in France, is the subject of multiple litigations in the United States and is wanted for questioning in Kazakhstan in relation to the murder of his predecessor at BTA Bank. Described by London's Evening Standard in December 2013 as 'the world's richest fugitive,' this is the astonishing story of Mukhtar Ablyazov.

Mukhtar Kabyluly Ablyazov

CHAPTER ONE

From Rags to Riches

Our story begins in the modest village of Galkino in the South Region of Kazakhstan on May 16th, 1963, when Mukhtar Kabyluly Ablyazov came into the world. The region, which shares its southern border with neighbouring Uzbekistan, is one of Kazakhstan's smallest but most densely populated and continues to grow, reflecting the economic climate. Much of the development over the last decade or so has come as a result of an influx of migrant workers, which includes many ethnic Kazakhs returning to their motherland.

One interesting demographic change has been the exodus of the ethnic Russian population that made up 23 percent of the population during the Soviet-era, a figure that now stands at just six percent. This is a change reflected across the former Soviet Union. During the time of Stalin, there was a policy of colonisation of the Soviet republics by ethnic Russians and Belarusians. This was usually preceded by a brutal process of ethnic cleansing.

Indeed, the artificially engineered famines of the 1930s known as 'Holodomor' that were targeted primarily at Ukraine, in which as many as seven million are believed to have perished, also affected Kazakhstan, where the loss of life could have been as high as one million. To this day, nobody is really sure about the numbers. During the final months no one was left to keep records, and for decades the Soviet regime made it a crime to even discuss Holodomor. Now, after several generations, it seems the last of the Russians are returning to their homeland as well.

To put the sheer scale of Kazakhstan in perspective, it is worth making a quick comparison. The South Region is one of the smallest but most populous parts of the country. It has an area of 117,248 square kilometres and a population of around two-and-a-half million people. That compares with Greater London, for example, that has an area of just 1,569 sq. km and a population of more than eight-and-a-half million.

Like all of Kazakhstan's regions, the south is blessed with an abundance of natural beauty and wildlife that is protected and managed effectively - one of the country's great strengths. It is in this environment that Ablyazov was born and raised and, while little information about his early life is in the public domain, it is clear that he was possessed of both considerable intelligence and ambition.

Ablyazov graduated from the Moscow Engineering Physics Institute in 1986 with a degree in theoretical physics. Taking Alma Shalabayeva as his wife the following year, he then went on to work as a junior researcher at the Kazakh National University, at that time called the Kazakh State University after the famous Soviet party leader, Sergei Kirov. Renamed in the 2000s, it became the Al-Farabi Kazakh National University.

In 1990, he enrolled in postgraduate studies, again at the Moscow Engineering Physics Institute, a move which resulted in the loss of his research job. This would appear to have been his impetus for entering the world of business, an exciting step at the time when the Soviet Union was entering its final days and opportunities were beginning to open up.

In 1991, after a short stint selling computers and photocopiers, Ablyazov registered his first company, which he named Madina after his eldest daughter. By the following year, he was supplying all the regions of Kazakhstan with foodstuffs and medicinal products. He established Astana Holding, a multi-sector private holding company that formed and consisted of Astana-Sugar, Astana-Food, Aral-Salt, The Shymkent Pasta Factory, Astana-Medical Service, Astana-Motors, Astana-Inter Hotel, Astana-Bank and the furniture business, Trade House Zhanna. This strategy of creating numerous private companies, which were not always obviously under his control, was one that Ablyazov quickly perfectly to his advantage.

In 1997, he was appointed as head of the state-owned Kazakhstan Electricity Grid Operating Company (KEGOC). After the arrival of Ablyazov, however, the company lost 12 percent of its revenues in the first year, whilst its expenses increased by 53 percent. The losses amassed by KEGOC in 1998 and the first quarter of 1999 amounted to nearly 20 million dollars. A similar situation occurred when Ablyazov was appointed as a general director of the national air carrier, Air Kazakhstan, which eventually filed for bankruptcy.

After just a year as head of KEGOC, Ablyazov was appointed Minister for Energy, Industry and Trade in the government of President Nazarbayev - a meteoric rise indeed. His career in Kazakhstan was to take one more twist, however, which would take the life of the entrepreneur and successful politician in an altogether different direction.

In 1998, together with a consortium of Kazakh investors, Ablyazov acquired a loan to buy shares in Bank Turan Alem, which was being sold in a privatisation auction for $72 million. The financial institution, later to be known as BTA Bank, was being set-up to become the victim of one of the greatest frauds in history; one that would include an allegation of murder.

Accident or Murder?

Yerzhan Tatishev, the head of BTA Bank, was killed in 2004 in what was described at the time as a 'hunting accident.' He died from a shot to the head whilst driving in a car with fellow hunters. The man responsible for his death, Muratkhan Tokmadi, a known criminal with strong links to organised crime, received a short jail sentence for causing Tatishev's 'death through negligence.'

The case did not end there, however. Following technical investigations into the weapon involved by experts from the United States and supported by witness testimonies, Tokmadi was to make a dramatic confession from his jail cell. In his new testimony, he described how Tatishev's death was no mere accident but a contract killing ordered by Mukhtar Ablyazov, who had succeeded Tatishev as head of the bank.

CHAPTER TWO

A Billionaire's Road to Britain

As he sat at his desk in his office as head of BTA Bank in Astana in 2009, Mukhtar Ablyazov embodied the image of an outstanding financial entrepreneur. Built upon his glorious financial achievements, however, this image was entirely false. Even as he worked, Ablyazov, known as one of the world's richest men, could not have failed to be aware that, despite his prestigious role as head of the bank, his standing was increasingly being undermined by his parallel reputation as the 'world's richest fraudster.' Certainly, he recognised that events were closing in on him and that his days at the bank were numbered.

A man described by former friends, rivals and law enforcement officers alike as a 'financial genius,' by this juncture Ablyazov had successfully embezzled a mind-blowing sum, believed to be as much as $7.6 billion from the bank which he had become head of shortly after the death of his predecessor. (A separate chapter is devoted to the story of Tatishev's murder.) Nobody really knows how much money went missing, only that it happened on Ablyazov's watch.

Between 2005 and 2009, Ablyazov had arranged for the issue of loans ostensibly obtained in order to finance real estate deals and other projects throughout the former Soviet Union. These loans were channelled through a web of shell companies. A reported $8 billion worth of such loans were approved, largely to entities operating out of mailboxes, holding no collateral and based in offshore tax havens. Ablyazov was subsequently found to have held significant anonymous ownership interests in more than one thousand such companies around the world. Funds were then transferred between these companies, often as loans which ended up with third-party entities from which the money could never be recovered.

In one particularly brazen transaction, a billion dollars was transferred from BTA to three companies in the oil and gas sector. This was done under the guise of loans for new drilling equipment to facilitate the exploration of the Mertviy Kultuk Oilfield in the Caspian Sea, said to hold reserves amounting to 154 million metric tons of crude oil. The type of equipment specified in the loan agreement, however, simply did not exist, and, unsurprisingly, no exploration took place.

Flight to England

Investigations following the financial crash of 2009 and Ablyazov's somewhat hurried departure from Kazakhstan revealed a massive 'blackhole' in the bank's accounts. Kazakhstan's sovereign wealth fund, the Samruk-Kazyna was obliged to inject funds to the tune of $10 billion into BTA in order to keep the institution solvent, becoming in the process its majority shareholder.

Britain's Royal Bank of Scotland, itself the recipient of a massive government bailout, was also a big loser in the BTA affair, having invested and lost some $1.8 billion of pension funds as a result of Ablyazov's activities. HSBC, Barclays, Morgan Stanley and Credit Suisse also suffered heavy losses.

Now a fugitive, Ablyazov disappeared from view, resurfacing in the UK, where he sought to take advantage of Britain's asylum system by presenting himself as a political refugee. His story was that in 2001 he had co-founded a political party, Democratic Choice of Kazakhstan (DCK), which, according to his strategy became his shield in cases of criminal prosecution for the frauds he had committed. In part, he succeeded.

Whilst in the position of Minister of Energy, Industry and Trade, Ablyazov had directed all of his talents into developing various schemes, considering the public service as an auxiliary tool for the expansion of his own business empire. Convicted in 2002 of 'abusing official powers,' he was sentenced to six years in prison. He served just ten months, however, before being freed after asking the Head of State for a pardon. Having been released, he reportedly spent 'millions of dollars funding opposition groups' from the safety of his new home, whilst claiming that his imprisonment had been an act of political repression.

On the basis of this presentation, he was successfully able to claim asylum in the UK, albeit temporarily. Portraying himself to the media as an 'innocent... victim of persecution' who was 'in fear of his life from his country's secret police, the KNB,' it was a story that journalists were ready to swallow, initially at least.

Ablyazov next set about building a considerable property portfolio in his new home country. Setting up base on Bishops Avenue – often referred to as 'Billionaire's Row' - in the leafy North London suburb of Hampstead, his neighbours included the late pop superstar, George Michael and the absentee Sultan of Brunei and Saudi royal family, who were rumoured at one point to have purchased a number of properties as 'boltholes' in case they should find themselves needing to make a hasty exit.

Ablyazov next purchased Carlton House for a cool £20 million. Glentree Estates of London, who handled the sale of Carlton House after Ablyazov's somewhat ignominious exit from the UK - which we will come to later - described it thus: 'The property is approached via a sweeping driveway allowing visitors the opportunity to fully appreciate the immense scale and quality of this impressive mansion. The understated architecture of the frontage gives little indication of the luxury and opulence that lies within including 7 bedrooms all with lavish marble en-suite bathrooms, an underground pool complex, a self-contained staff apartment and even a 10-person Turkish bath. An impressive entrance hall with sweeping marble and wrought iron staircase welcomes visitors to Carlton House. A series of magnificent reception rooms lead off from the hall including a sitting room, a 50ft drawing room/ballroom, a family room, a private study and a dining room offering unlimited potential for grand entertaining.'

Many of the properties on Bishops Avenue are currently owned by offshore companies. This not only ensures the anonymity of the actual owners - rumours of kings and presidents, superstars and mafia godfathers abound in Hampstead - but also means that expensive stamp duty does not have to be paid when these properties are bought and sold in line with current UK law. The super-rich do not like paying taxes.

With one prestigious home in London not being enough, Ablyazov also acquired a £1 million apartment in upmarket St John's Wood, close to Lord's Cricket Ground. It is not known if he is a fan of the game, but cricket has recently garnered some interest in Kazakhstan. In 2007, Wisden Cricketers' Almanack reported the existence of Almaty cricket club, which at the time boasted 15 regulars and played on the tarmac on the premises of School No. 130. As it maintains a Facebook page, the club has clearly lasted the course.

For all their grandeur and fine locations, though, these properties were eclipsed by Ablyazov's less than modest 100-acre estate at Oakland Park in Berkshire. The estate boasts eight houses and a private helipad situated conveniently close to the prestigious Oakland Park Golf Club, in close proximity to Windsor Castle, Her Majesty Queen Elizabeth II's favourite home. It is unclear how much he paid for this property; contemporary reports vary from £18-20 million.

The English Courts Weigh In

Of course, not every political refugee can afford such a luxurious lifestyle, surrounded by security personnel to protect him or her from ruthless political enemies, real or imagined. But this idyllic English sojourn was about to come to a sudden and dramatic end as an English court was set to deprive Ablyazov of his impressive property portfolio.

BTA Bank had issued eleven writs against Ablyazov for a total of $6 billion, and as a result, he was ordered by an English court to repay the value of securities illegally transferred by him to his companies in the British Virgin Islands. A subsequent freezing order forbade Ablyazov from seeking to 'in any way dispose of, deal with or diminish the value of any of his assets in England and Wales up to the value of... £451,130,000.'

With Ablyazov having failed to comply with this order, in February 2012, High Court Judge Mr Justice Teare handed down a sentence of twenty two months' imprisonment for contempt of court. 'I do not consider that anything less would mark the seriousness of Mr Ablyazov's conduct in failing to comply with the freezing order,' he said in his judgement.

With all this hanging over him, the fugitive Ablyazov had already decided that it was time to make another hasty and discreet exit. Having had enough experience of Ablyazov to appreciate the measure of the man, by this juncture the English courts had ordered that he be placed on a ports 'watch list' prior to sentencing. Despite his photograph being displayed at airports and ports, he slipped through the net. Apparently, he left on a bus to France using, it is presumed, a false passport.

Between November 2012 and March 2013, the English courts were to pass a total of $4.2 billion in judgments against Ablyazov. As Lord Justice Maurice Kay observed, 'it is difficult to imagine a party to commercial litigation who has acted with more cynicism, opportunism and deviousness towards court orders than Mr Ablyazov.' Only a small fraction of this money has been recovered, what has been coming from the sale of Ablyazov's former properties in the UK.

Warrants for Ablyazov's arrest issued in Kazakhstan, Russia and Ukraine remain outstanding. The three countries are seeking his extradition to answer multiple charges. A Red Notice issued against him by Interpol was controversially rescinded following pressure from a somewhat dubious human rights Non-Governmental Organisation (NGO) with the backing of a handful of members of the European Parliament. Ablyazov has also been the subject of two drawn-out civil court cases in New York and California, alleging that he and his relative by marriage, former Mayor of Almaty, Viktor Khrapunov made investments in real estate and businesses in the US using stolen money.

On June 7th 2017, a court in Almaty convicted Ablyazov in absentia of organising and leading a criminal group, abuse of office, embezzlement and financial mismanagement. He received a 20-year jail sentence. Dismissing the verdict, Ablyazov said: 'I do not care what sort of decision they are making there about me, because this trial is false.' He is reported to have instructed his legal team not to challenge the court's ruling.

Partners in Crime

In December 2016, the England and Wales Court of Appeal considered allegations that an associate of Ablyazov, Viktor Khrapunov's son-in-law, Ilyas, who along with members of his family had found sanctuary in Switzerland, had conspired with Ablyazov to breach the asset freezing order laid down by Justice Teare in the High Court. The judge held that the bank has 'a good arguable case in conspiracy against Mr Khrapunov to the requisite standard on the basis of his and Mr Ablyazov's alleged breaches of the freezing order and the receivership order... Mr Khrapunov has not filed any evidence to deny that he has indeed assisted Mr Ablyazov in seeking to avoid the effect of the worldwide freezing order against him and the receivership order in the ways alleged by the Bank.'

Viktor Khrapunov is, at the time of writing, on Interpol's Red List. He is wanted in connection with the 'Creation and Guidance of an Organised Criminal Group or Criminal Association (Criminal Organisation) and Participation in a Criminal Association; Expropriation or Embezzlement of Trusted Property; Fraud; Legalisation of Monetary Funds or Other Property Obtained Illegally; Abuse of Official Powers and Receipt of a Bribe.'

Khrapunov's son, Ilyas, who just happens to be married to Mukhtar Ablyazov's daughter and firstborn, Madina, is also subject to multiple extradition warrants and is, like his father, on Interpol's Red List. In addition to the usual fraud, corruption and organised criminal activities associated with this extended family, Ilyas Khrapunov is wanted in Ukraine to answer charges of computer hacking, a criminal offence in that country. In March 2018, it was reported that the Geneva Canton Public Prosecutor's Office had launched an investigation into members of the Khrapunov family on charges of 'legalisation of assets obtained by stealing the property of the city of Almaty.'

With its tentacles even reaching into Trump Tower and the institutions of the European Union, the scale of the criminal network surrounding Ablyazov becomes ever more apparent as the story unfolds. In the meantime, we follow the fugitive from justice to France.

Flawed Judgement

Mukhtar Ablyazov's decision to flee to the UK was, with hindsight, most probably a deeply flawed one. The country has sympathetic asylum laws and a record of providing safe haven to political dissidents from the former Soviet republics. But many of the fake companies Ablyazov had established for the purpose of funnelling BTA Bank assets out of Kazakhstan were based in the British Virgin Islands and came under the jurisdiction of the English courts. This led to the November 2012 judgement ordering Ablyazov to pay over £1 billion plus interest and 'new post-judgment asset-freezing orders made against Mr Ablyazov in an unlimited sum and new asset-freezing orders in relation to certain other defendants.'

It was his breach of this freezing order that resulted in the twenty-two-month jail sentence for contempt of court, having lied, in the words of High Court Justice Teare in a 'deliberate, substantial and brazen way' about his ownership of companies and property. Ablyazov clearly reasoned that another flight from justice was his best option, and so he hightailed it to France.

By this point, he had a good many people on his trail. No less than four governments, Interpol, and significant private interests, including the BTA Bank, were actively pursuing him. The British-based firm, Diligence, that specialises in complex cross-border inquiries and whose operatives are primarily former spies and ex-special forces had been trailing Ablyazov's friends and associates since his arrival in the UK.

*Ablyavov's apartment in London's exclusive
St. John's Wood*

*Carlton House, Ablyazov's £20 million home
in Bishops Avenue, London - known locally
as "Billionaire's Row"*

CHAPTER THREE

The Move to France

Ablyazov was a wanted man; could he really find refuge in France? His flight there certainly exposed him to significant risk. On January 6th, 2013, a French judge ordered the now acknowledged fraudster to be extradited to Russia, where he was facing criminal charges in relation to his activities at BTA Bank. Ablyazov had spent a considerable amount of his life in Moscow and was well aware of the reception he would face at the hands of Federal Security Service (FSB) Interrogators. The successor to the KGB, Vladimir Putin was Director of the FSB from July 1998 to August 1999, and it is, like the fictional James Bond, licensed to kill at home or abroad.

Ablyazov went underground, but in July 2013 his enemies were to catch up with him in a series of dramatic and somewhat entertaining escapades. What was to occur would not have been out of place in an Ian Fleming novel or, indeed, one of the saucy British Carry On franchise comedies.

An important player in Ablyazov's life at this juncture was the 37-year-old Olena Tyshchenko, a Ukrainian lawyer and mother of four whose name whenever she is mentioned in the tabloids is usually pre-ceded by the words 'glamorous blonde.' Tyshchenko was one of those under close observation by private investigators representing the interests of BTA Bank. On Monday, July 22nd of that year, Tyshchenko attended a High Court hearing in London related to BTA's case against Ablyazov. Successfully obtaining an adjournment, she left the court, but unbeknownst to her, she was about to lead a team of investigators from the court to Ablyazov's hideout in France in circumstances that would come as a complete surprise to the sleuths themselves.

Hailing a taxi to Heathrow Airport, Tyshchenko flew to Nice in the South of France, where she spent time shopping before continuing to a villa to join her children. Having trailed her to the villa where she arrived at 1.30am, the investigators prepared themselves for a long night of surveillance. Events soon took an unexpected turn, however, when an hour later she emerged from the property having changed into 'a short skirt and high heels.' Tyshchenko then drove to the Villa Neptune in Miramar, a high-end location on the French Riviera owned by her husband, the Ukrainian businessman and former executive of Ukraine's Fortuna Bank, Sergei Tyshchenko, a former partner of Ablyazov.

Capitalising on their unexpected good fortune, investigators took up positions offering vantage points from which to continue their surveillance. They were to meet with a great unexpected boon. Through a window, they spotted Mukhtar Ablyazov wearing only his boxer shorts and carefully rearranging the covers of a double bed strewn with lilies.

Tyshchenko stayed for what was left of the night and left the villa at about noon before returning later that same day. Ablyazov's car was observed leaving the Villa Neptune on the evening of Friday, July 26th, from where he drove to the Villa Saint Basile at Mougins in the Alpes-Maritimes department of south-eastern France, located on the heights overlooking Cannes. Tyshchenko followed him there, and they again spent the night together.

By Monday 29th, BTA Bank officials, acting on the information they had received, contacted the French authorities to inform them of

Ablyazov's whereabouts, pointing out that the fugitive was the subject of an Interpol Red Notice and multiple extradition requests. On Tuesday 30th, under close observation by the private investigation team and the French security services, with the net closing around him, Ablyazov travelled to a third villa, the Chemin de Castellaras at Mouans-Sartoux.

The next day, fifteen police officers mounted an armed raid. A helicopter equipped with thermal imaging cameras hovered overhead in case the oligarch tried to make a run for it. Amid totally unfounded rumours that he was protected by armed men, the small 'private army' of arresting officers was backed up by French Special Forces. In the event, Ablyazov, who had been working at his computer and was dressed in casual T-shirt and shorts submitted quietly and calmly to his arrest shortly before 2 pm. An 18-month manhunt had come to an end.

Appearing in court in Aix-en-Provence the following day, he was detained pending extradition proceedings. BTA Managing Director, Pavel Prosyankin welcomed Ablyazov's arrest, saying after the court appearance that the bank was 'optimistic' about recovering 'more of the assets which the courts have authorised us to seize' to compensate for the missing billions they claimed Ablyazov was responsible for.

Although France has no extradition agreement with Kazakhstan, it does with both Russia and Ukraine. Hence, Ablyazov was ordered by a lower court to be extradited. Following an appeal by Ablyazov's legal team, this decision was upheld on March 4th, 2014 by France's Cour de Cassation. 'I am extremely disappointed because I think there is a real problem if Mr Ablyazov is sent back to Russia or Ukraine,' Ablyazov's lawyer, Claire Waquet was reported to have said at the time. Ablyazov's wife, Alma Shalabayeva, claimed that he faced being sent to Kazakhstan if was extradited under the order, which had been signed by the then French Prime Minister, Manuel Valls.

CHAPTER FOUR

The Deportation of Shalabayeva

Alma Shalabayeva herself had been controversially deported from Italy to Kazakhstan in 2013, along with her six-year-old daughter, Alua. Whilst searching for her husband, whom they believed to be hiding out in a villa in Rome, the Italian police found Alma to be in possession of what they described as a 'fake' Central African Republic (CAR) passport. Shalabayeva's lawyers claimed that she had been kidnapped under the deportation procedure as the CAR passport was genuine. This was later confirmed by the country's government.

Ablyazov was also in possession of a CAR diplomatic passport issued in the name of Marat Ayan. This was the document that he is believed to have used during his escape from British justice in 2012. It is not known if the issuing of diplomatic passports in fake names is standard practice in the CAR, nor indeed what such a service might cost. Nor is it known what diplomatic services the Ablyazov family might have rendered to the impoverished nation, but in certain circles, it is clear that anything can be had at a price.

The deportation of Shalabayeva caused a great deal of controversy in Italy. It had occurred under unusual circumstances involving a swift police operation and a flight to Kazakhstan on a private jet. The press and some opposition politicians accused the government of circumventing legal and diplomatic processes with the aim of garnering goodwill from the government of the oil and mineral-rich Central Asian country. The UN Human Rights Office raised its own concerns with Italy over the expulsion of Shalabayeva and her daughter, saying it amounted to an 'extraordinary rendition' and that she faced possible persecution in Kazakhstan on account of her husband's political activities.

As a result of this outcry, Italy requested the return of the deportees from Kazakhstan, a request to which the government in Astana readily agreed. The family were duly returned to Rome on Friday, December 13th, where they were welcomed by Italy's Foreign Minister, Emma Bonino. An official photograph showed the minister with her arm around Shalabayeva's waist and her hand affectionately placed on Alua's head. 'It was a pleasure for me to be able to share with Mrs Shalabayeva and her children their joy at being here in Rome again,' Bonino said in a statement.

Whilst all these events were taking place, Ablyazov was languishing in the notorious Fleury-Mérogis Prison on the outskirts of Paris. With 4,100 inmates, it is the largest prison in Europe and is recognised to be a hotbed of Islamic radicalisation. Riots within the prison walls are often suppressed with tear gas and baton charges. Often described as 'dysfunctional' at best, the French prison system has one of the highest suicide rates in Europe.

For Ablyazov, the Fleury-Mérogis Prison would have felt a very long way from Billionaire's Row in London, or the Tyshchenko villa in the Cote d'Azur with all their creature comforts. The fear of extradition to Russia, which was waiting for approval by governmental decree, however, and what might happen to him when he landed in Moscow, would have been weighing far more heavily on his mind.

As for Olena Tyshchenko, soon after Ablyazov's arrest and subsequent incarceration, she was to hit the headlines herself. Having represented his interests in the Royal Courts of Justice in London and led investigators to the French hideaway owned by her husband, her association with Ablyazov was already beyond question. Furthermore, with her husband having named the fugitive in his divorce petition, she was becoming increasingly implicated in his criminal activities.

The Arrest and Rehabilitation of Olena Tyshchenko

During one of her frequent trips to Moscow, on August 30th, 2013, Tyshchenko was placed under arrest by the Russian authorities on suspicion of large-scale fraud and the laundering of more than $3.3 billion in illegally obtained funds. To be precise, she was accused of legalising the monies under two articles of Russia's Criminal Code: 159, 'Very Serious Fraud,' and 174.1, 'Legalisation of Stolen Funds'.

All allegations against Tyshchenko stemmed directly from the period during which she was representing Ablyazov. Russian investigators believed that she was responsible for covering up all traces of Ablyazov's money-laundering schemes during his time as head of BTA Bank and making illegally obtained assets appear as if they were legally procured. She was held for four months before being released under an amnesty which became possible after BTA Bank withdrew its claim for $439 million in damages. Following her release, she returned to Ukraine in early 2014, and in May of that year was appointed as head of the presidential administration's interdepartmental working group on anti-corruption legislation.

Then, on July 7th, 2015 it was announced that Tyshchenko - who was credited as having nine years of experience on the committee on corruption of the Verkhovna Rada, the Ukrainian Parliament, despite having worked in that role for less than a year - had been chosen to head the Ministry of the Interior's efforts to recover Ukrainian assets illegally moved overseas.

Unsurprisingly, Tyshchenko's appointment proved highly controversial and triggered a flood of criticism. On July 10th, 2015 the Kyiv Post reported on rumours that Tyshchenko had been given the job only because of her former husband's ties to Serhiy Pashinsky, then acting head of the presidential administration. This was something that Pashinsky himself denied. 'As far as I know, Tania Chornovol engaged Olena Tyshchenko as an expert into drawing up the law, and I see no problems here,' he responded when asked by a journalist how Olena Tyshchenko, who had allegedly been involved in money laundering, could possibly be deemed a fit chief for the interdepartmental anti-corruption legislation task force.

At that time of Tyshchenko's initial appointment, Ms Chornovol was a senior official responsible for anti-corruption efforts, a post she would subsequently resign from citing her frustration at the lack of progress in tackling corruption by the Ukrainian Government and characterising those who sought to stymie these efforts as 'hyenas.'

'Out of nine years of service to the state, Tyshchenko spent eight years not serving the state at all, but in London, France and in a Moscow detention facility,' wrote Ukrainian parliamentarian, Serhiy Leshchenko. 'And now she will be responsible for cooperating with Western security services in recovering stolen assets. Do you not find that ridiculous?' A former investigative journalist, Leshchenko was a central figure in revelations relating to the scandals surrounding former Trump campaign head, Paul Manafort and his myriad connections with former Ukrainian President, Viktor Yanukovych.

Despite the media furore, announcing the appointment Interior Minister, Arsen Avakov praised Tyshchenko as a 'remarkable individual' with vast professional experience. Tyshchenko's appointment within the Ministry of the Interior, as with her previous appointment to the working group on anti-corruption legislation in 2014, was clouded by controversy and speculation surrounding the activities and possible influence of her former husband.

According to a report in Ukrainska Pravda in May of that same year, which cited a document sent by the Security Service of Ukraine (SBU) to the Prosecutor General's Office, the SBU suspected Serhiy Tyshchenko of involvement in a scheme to embezzle over 85,000 tonnes of oil products. The SBU identified the products as belonging to the tycoon, Serhiy Kurchenko, an ally of ousted President Viktor Yanukovych, and they were seized by the government during an investigation into a smuggling case.

Despite all this, Artyom Shevchenko, a spokesman for the ministry told the Kyiv Post that Olena Tyshchenko was chosen for the job based on her professional merits and that her ties to her ex-husband and previous involvement with Ablyazov 'would not influence her effectiveness' in recovering stolen assets. 'The appointment was made considering her ability to get results in recovering stolen assets. In this sphere, she is very competent, and I think we will see good results from her work,' he commented.

According to a popular idiom, 'it takes a thief to catch a thief'. Was Olena Tyshchenko a 'poacher turned gamekeeper?' Or was it the case that the political elite in Ukraine, a country in which the corruption of political institutions is institutionalised, saw in Tyshchenko a slick and well-connected operator with exactly the skills they need in order to cover their own tracks?

Whilst Tyshchenko had gone from a Russian jail to a Ukrainian ministry, her former client and lover - if that description accurately reflects the situation - was still staring at the grim walls of his prison cell. He was, however, about to receive some very good news.

Ablyazov Walks Free From Jail

Late on the evening of Friday, December 9th, 2016, after spending years behind bars, Mukhtar Ablyazov walked free from jail, hugging his 24-year-old son, Madiyar in the company of his brother and his Canadian lawyer, Peter Sahlas. 'We are thrilled with the result today,' said Sahlas, who had worked on Ablyazov's case since his initial arrival in London; 'this is a huge step forward for human rights law in France and Europe.'

Earlier that day, the French Council of State had annulled the extradition order against Ablyazov, judging that the request from Russia was politically motivated. 'Mr Ablyazov is an opponent of the political regime in Kazakhstan and has been recognised as a political refugee by the British authorities,' the Conseil d'Etat said in a statement that was somewhat flawed, as the British government had revoked Ablyazov's refugee status.

Ablyazov's defence team had concentrated their efforts on their client's political activities, arguing that he was being pursued because of his activities as an opposition leader in Kazakhstan. His defence team had contended that he would not get a fair trial in Russia and that he faced the risk of being extradited to Kazakhstan. Their arguments enjoyed the support of the UN's Special Rapporteur on Torture and Other Cruel, Inhuman or Degrading Treatment or Punishment, Nils Melzer. The defence team's emphasis in court on Ablyazov as a 'victim of political repression' had propelled them to victory.

CHAPTER FIVE

Criminal Networks

To understand the sheer scale of the activities of the network Mukh-tar Ablyazov had created, it is necessary to look at some of those involved. Ablyazov had built up a vast nexus of criminal associates as his activities spread. Of these, Viktor Khrapunov is almost certainly the most central and was named as such in the High Court of England and Wales. Formerly the Mayor of Almaty - the then capital of Kazakhstan - he faces, at the time of writing, multiple allegations of corruption, fraud and money laundering in his home country and abroad. His track record shares a number of similarities with his fellow fugitive and partner in crime, Ablyazov.

Viktor Vyacheslavovich Khrapunov was born in 1948 in the relatively modest surroundings of the village of Pryedgornoye in the north-east of Kazakhstan. His parents were both civil servants. His father had been seriously wounded during the Second World War, known as the Great Patriotic War in the former Soviet republics, and was an invalid.

After completing his studies at the Industrial College in Ust-Kamenogorsk, the young Khrapunov set out to seek his fortune in Almaty. Working first as a repair mechanic, then as a foreman and later as a senior engineer at the Almaty Thermal Power Station, he studied part-time at the Almaty Power Engineering Institute. It was during his college years that he took his first step on the path to a career in the political arena by joining Komsomol, the youth league of the Communist Party.

Attaining the office of Chairman of the Almaty Lenin District Communist Party Committee, he was soon promoted to the post of First Deputy Chair of the Almaty City Council. He eventually reached the position of Chairman of the Executive Committee of the City Soviet of People's Deputies that came under the direct authority of the all-Union Supreme Soviet.

Following the collapse of the Soviet Union and Kazakhstan's subsequent independence, Khrapunov continued his work at the Almaty municipality as First Deputy Mayor until 1995. There then followed periods in high office, first as Minister of Energy and Coal, and subsequently as Minister of Energy and Natural Resources. This rise through the corridors of power was to come to a temporary halt when the economic turbulence experienced by Kazakhstan in the mid-1990s led to the downfall of Prime Minister, Akezhan Kazhegeldin along with most of his cabinet ministers.

In 1997, Khrapunov became the Mayor of Almaty, and in 2004 he was appointed as Governor of the East Kazakhstan Province, a position he was to hold until 2007 when he was appointed Minister of Emergency Measures in the country's cabinet. That same year, he announced his withdrawal from all public functions and his retirement for 'health reasons.'

Eventually, Khrapunov was to become implicated in wide-scale fraud. He has been the subject of no less than twenty criminal prosecutions and was found guilty of defrauding the Kazakh state to the tune of some $300 million. Like his associate Ablyazov, he had created interesting methods for transferring money from Kazakhstan to his own purse, but in the United States, Khrapunov was to run into big problems.

Viktor Khrapunov - Justice Teare in the High Court of England & Wales stated that BTA Bank has a "good arguable case of conspiracy" against him, & that "Mr Khrapunov has not filed any evidence to deny that he has indeed assisted Mr Ablyazov in seeking to avoid the effect of the worldwide freezing order against him..

CHAPTER SIX

The Trump Connection

The US Government, having verified allegations made by the Ka
zakh authorities, put blocks on a number of properties, including several
belonging to Khrapunov and his family that it was alleged were acquired
with laundered money. Generally, ownership of such real estate is not
directly in the name of Khrapunov but by way of beneficial ownership,
entities such as offshore companies. Consequently, the authorities have
taken some time to find evidence of real estate transactions with which
he may have been involved in the US. Khrapunov appears to have used at
least three companies - Soho 3310, Soho 3311 and Soho 3203 - to move
money from Kazakhstan. Since each of these entities is a limited liability
company, it is easy to hide the real owner.

A week after the companies were created in April 2013 in New York,
property records show they paid a total of $3.1 million to buy apart-
ments in the 46-storey luxury hotel condominium, Trump SoHo, com-
pleted in 2010 in a chic corner of Manhattan. The US authorities also
discovered that the ultimate beneficiary of the three companies was Elvira
Kudryashova, Khrapunov's daughter. She had engaged the New York law
firm Martin Jajan to handle the transactions, with Mr Jajan himself si-
gning the purchase documents on behalf of the Soho companies in the
capacity of the buyer's agent.

The vendor of the properties was the New York-based company, Bayrock/Sapir Organization LLC. This is the entity that links Ablyazov's money through the Khrapunovs with Donald Trump. It was named after the developers that jointly built Trump SoHo, namely the Sapir Organisation, founded by the Georgian, Tamir Sapir, and Bayrock, founded by Tevfik Arif, a Kazakhstan-born former Soviet official. According to regulatory filings, Bayrock/Sapir Organization LLC had a third co-owner - Donald Trump, the man who licensed his personal brand to the project and who would become US President.

Khrapunov was the owner of the Swiss Development Group (SDG), an entity created with money laundered out of Kazakhstan. The Geneva-based company - the one allegedly used to violate British court orders freezing Mukhtar Ablyazov's assets - was looking for investment projects and seeking financing. For such projects, funds would have been drawn from Kazakhstan, Russia and Ukraine, where the branches of the BTA Bank under Ablyazov's control were located.

As has been mentioned, the ostensible business connections between Viktor Khrapunov and Mukhtar Ablyazov extend to their families: Khrapunov's son, Ilyas, is married to Ablyazov's daughter, Madina. However, there appears to have initially been some reticence on the part of Ablyazov over the union. Zhaksylyk Zharimbetov, former Deputy Chairman of BTA's management board, chair of the bank's loan committee and number two to Ablyazov, who fled the country with the fugitive before returning to Kazakhstan in 2017, revealed as much in an interview. 'As far as I know, Mukhtar was very bad with Khrapunov,' he said. 'He considered him a grabber and corrupt. Even he [Ablyazov] said that one day, when there was a government meeting, he almost got into a fight with him. Naturally, when his daughter told him that she was marrying Khrapunov's son he took it painfully. Over time, he certainly resigned himself and (Ilyas) Khrapunov became a member of the family.

'He [Ablyazov] is certainly very smart. He has good organisational skills; he is focused and consistent in achieving his goals. But at the same time he is conceited and self-centred. He uses people but then he throws them away. He is merciless; he is one of those people who will neither regret themselves nor others to achieve their own goals. Ablyazov talks about the problems in the country but as far as I can see his main goal is to seize power in the country. When we were in London we spent a lot of time together. He said that while in Kazakhstan he communicated with fortune-tellers. His mother is apparently addicted to this and through her he got to know them. They told him: "You will be a padishah! (emperor)." Then I asked him: "Do you believe in this?" He replied that he believed. I realised that he is obsessed, he wants to come to power by any means.'

Zharimbetov is rumoured to be preparing to go public on further details of this and other events in a forthcoming book.

Ilyas Khrapunov was educated in Switzerland at the exclusive Institut Le Rosey, which has the distinction of being the world's most expensive boarding school with annual fees in the region of $150,000. He also enjoys Swiss citizenship. According to John Lennon and Paul McCartney, money can't buy love, but a Swiss passport is something else altogether. Companies under his control - allegedly bolstered by Ablyazov's money - have facilitated the implementation of a number of very large and prestigious real estate projects; these include Kempinski Park, Chardon residence, 51 SPA Residence in Leukerbad, Pinnacle residence in Saas Fee, Switzerland, the Hotel Iglo in France and developments under the banner of real estate specialists, Rockefeller Estates. Through such means, it appears that stolen funds have been turned into highly valuable "clean" properties, including five-star condominium hotels and private hotels in Switzerland and other countries.

Ilyas Khrapunov turned SDG into a machine for laundering his father-in-law's wealth, according to a sworn statement filed in court by Nicolas Bourg, a Belgian businessman who had worked at the company. In that statement from 2016, Bourg stated that Khrapunov had directed him to set up a real estate fund as an SDG subsidiary and create a series of investment entities in Luxembourg that all answered to Khrapunov and, ultimately, to Ablyazov. Whilst Khrapunov Jr. denied the allegations, according to a lawsuit filed at the federal court in New York in 2015 by the City of Almaty and BTA Bank, he also helped to launder the $300 million that his father is accused of embezzling when he was mayor of Almaty. Like his father, Ilyas Khrapunov has long been sought by Interpol for money laundering, fraud, the organisation of a criminal group, abuse of authority and corruption. Like his father-in-law, he is also the subject of multiple extradition warrants.

It was in around 2008 that Khrapunov Jr. first met Felix Sater, a Russian born New York-based adviser to Donald Trump, who helped to attract investment into the Trump property portfolio. With his broad Brooklyn accent, Sater is said to have enjoyed an affable relationship with Donald Trump, although Trump claims to have no recollection of the man whatsoever.

Sater, whose family name used to be Saterov according to his sister, is a controversial character to say the least. When it suits his ends, he is keen to play down his Russian background by emphasising his Jewish roots. Sater was born in Moscow in 1966, so his birth certificate would state 'Jew' as the nationality of his father, Mikhail Sheferovsky, who has convictions for extorting money from restaurants, grocery stores and medical clinics. He has claimed that his family left the USSR when he was six years of age in order to escape political persecution and anti-Semitism. This book is, it may be wryly noted, full of known and alleged criminals who are claiming to be on the run in order to escape 'political persecution.'

Sater's early career as a stockbroker came to an abrupt end in 1991; he lost his license after smashing a Margherita glass into the face of a man in a bar brawl in Manhattan, causing serious injuries. Found guilty of first-degree assault, he spent fifteen months in the minimum-security Edgecombe Correctional Facility in New York City.

In 1998, Sater was convicted of fraud related to a $40 million operation conducted by the Russian Mafia that involved his company, White Rock Partners. Making a plea deal, he agreed to assist the FBI and federal prosecutors, thereby becoming an informer. In return, he received a $25,000 fine but served no jail time. His court records were sealed for ten years by order of Loretta Lynch, then the US Attorney for the Eastern District of New York.

Sater denies that he was ever informing on the mafia. 'I have never been a mafia informant ever in my life,' he told Britain's Guardian newspaper via email in 2017. 'I was a co-operating witness on my 1998 Wall street case as where [sic] fifteen other defendants [in] that case [which] basically ended in 2000. My work with various US government agencies both before the 1998 case as well as for over [two] decades after was in the area of National Security and did not include any mafia members of any kind.'

In 2003, Sater had joined the New York-based Bayrock Group, founded by Kazakh businessman Tevfik Arif in 2001 and later to become one half of Bayrock/Sapir Organization LLC, an international real estate development and investment company based out of New York. Arif had started out by developing property in Brooklyn, running Bayrock single-handedly before taking on Sater as managing director.

It was after Arif moved his company to Trump Tower and he developed a business relationship with Donald Trump that led to a licensing deal for the Trump Soho Hotel that his business really took off. In 2007, he traded future profits for a number of Trump's projects in return for

$50 million in financing from the Icelandic company, FL group. Bayrock was also to help develop the Trump International Hotel and Tower in Fort Lauderdale, Florida, as well as projects in Turkey, Poland, Ukraine and Russia. From around 2004, Arif and Sater were also working to introduce Trump to investors from Russia.

During this time, the pair were regularly travelling to Moscow and to the Cote d'Azur, charming Russian oligarchs in pursuit of investments into Trump-branded property projects. According to US court documents, in 2008 Bayrock partnered with Khrapunov's SDG for a major project to turn the Hotel du Parc on Lake Geneva into twenty-four luxury residences. Between them, the Khrapunov family purchased three condos in Trump SoHo for a combined total of $3.2 million.

Investments in the US continued, and by 2013 an SDG subsidiary called Triadou had invested $114 million in a number of projects, none of them believed to be associated with Trump. Along with Arif and Sater, Khrapunov Jr. appears to have been the main interface for the family in a relationship that was eventually to connect Ablyazov's money to Donald Trump.

Court Judgement Against Ilyas Khrapunov: Trump Implicated

In August 2018, the High Court of England and Wales ruled that Ilyas Khrapunov had conspired with Mukhtar Ablyazov to swindle over $6 billion. Court documents openly suggest that some of this vast sum is likely to have been laundered through the real estate empire of US President Donald Trump. Khrapunov had enlisted the assistance of a Dubai-based second generation British-Indian accountant by the name of Eesh Aggarwal to break the freezing order against Ablyazov, the judgment stated, ordering him to pay BTA around $500 million in damages.

'Mr Aggarwal was an English accountant, but well-versed in making use of offshore companies and other entities by which the true ownership of particular assets could be concealed,' the judgment reads. 'Mr Aggarwal provided services to Mr Khrapunov, and Mr Khrapunov told Mr Aggarwal he was acting on behalf of a number of clients, but did not reveal the truth, which was that his true client was in fact Mr Ablyazov.'

Kenes Rakishev, Chairman of the Board of Directors of BTA Bank told Newsweek that 'Mukhtar Ablyazov has been hiding behind a smokescreen of self-styled political dissidence in his efforts to evade international justice. This ruling from the British High Court is a significant step towards recovering more than $6 billion embezzled by Mr Ablyazov and his co-conspirators.'

Interpol's Red Notice on Ilyas Khrapunov - the charges against him are remarkably similar to those against his father, Viktor.

*Bota Jardemalie, named as Ablyazov's "right hand",
seen hear on her wedding day.*

CHAPTER SEVEN

Viktor Khrapunov's Retirement

Viktor Khrapunov may now officially be retired and living comfortably in Switzerland, but he appears to have returned to the political arena under the banner 'Democratic Khrapunov'. He now pontificates on the state of democracy in his native country, seemingly advocating a form of governance based on the Swiss system for Kazakhstan. A line that appears on his official website states that Khrapunov 'supports all policies that empower individuals to take an active role in modelling their own future. He believes Switzerland to be a model for emerging democracies.'

This admiration of Switzerland is understandable as it is the country where he and his family reside in safely today, a nation where they are among the richest residents with their considerable wealth based on money and valuables 'sent' from Kazakhstan. 'Democratic Khrapunov' may, however, be nothing more than a convenient shroud. By returning to politics, if only nominally, Khrapunov Sr. has repositioned himself as an opposition politician, a tactic that has worked so well for Ablyazov in avoiding extradition.

Bota Jardemalie: Ablyazov's 'Right Hand'

The woman who has been described as Mukhtar Ablyazov's 'right hand' at BTA Bank, in 2005, the year he became head of BTA, Botagoz Jardemalie was recruited by Ablyazov to become a member of the management board. Almost from day one, she was to prove unpopular with her colleagues, especially the females. 'As a lawyer, Botagoz Jardemalie was good, but the bank had many such, and many even better,' a former colleague said in an interview with the German website EU Chronicle. 'So how did she rise so quickly to the board of BTA Bank? By her bosom in Ablyazov's office, but certainly not with his mind. She is far from being stupid, she received a good education.

'She is from an academic family, and was well trained. On the human side, while she had been working in BTA, Jardemalie showed her worst. She was always self-assured, but if she could not achieve something by herself, then she did it through Ablyazov, behind the backs of others. Because of her efforts, the bank lost three of its most promising women professionals.'

Jardemalie is alleged to have been personally involved in illegal loans issued by BTA Bank worth approximately $500 million, presumably made to some of the more than 1,000 companies set up by or on behalf of Ablyazov that apparently were never repaid. She is said to have personally put pressure on the BTA's Credit Committee and to have overseen "investment projects" that were part of the money-laundering scheme.

In 2009, like her former boss and, according to the Kazakh press, her former lover Ablyazov, she fled Kazakhstan, relocating to Belgium. In a by now familiar move, she claimed 'political persecution' and on that basis received the status of a political refugee, presenting herself as a 'human rights defender.' Allegedly extremely wealthy, she found a home in the leafy Brussels suburb of Uccle, an area favoured by highly paid Eurocrats and home to one of the prestigious EU Commission funded European Schools.

Shortly after her arrival in Belgium, Jardemalie founded a company, Botagoz Jardemalie SPRL, offering consultancy on cross-border litigation cases and managing lucrative projects developed between the European Union and Kazakhstan. Intriguingly, her business address in Schaerbeek, Brussels, was also that of the law firm, Ruchat Lexial, founded by Emmanuel Ruchat, a well-connected expert in immigration issues, criminal and political law.

In March 2013, her company changed its name to Ponte Mundi, and in February 2016 it was sold to Ruchat Lexial, with Jardemalie being appointed to the position of managing director. In September 2016, Jardemalie resigned from her position and shortly thereafter the company was sold to two Lebanese businessmen, Fadi Abdul Had and Mazen Hawwa, both originally hailing from Beirut but giving addresses in Kuwait.

Money Laundering Allegations

This transaction, and the very fact of involvement with Lebanon might appear highly dubious given that it is associated with a person who stands accused of embezzlement and has been closely associated with others accused of money laundering. Supporting such suspicions, in 2017 it was reported that the Belgian judiciary was conducting an investigation against Jardemalie on allegations of laundering some $100 million in that country.

Also under investigation for money laundering on behalf of Mukhtar Ablyazov over the 'disappearance' of about $647,000 of funds relating to a company called SKY Service LLP which he controlled is Jardemalie's brother, Iskander Yerimbetov. In fact, there is a process for fraud involving more than $610,000, the victims of which are seven legal entities. The defendants, Sky Service LLP, allegedly charged an inflated fee for air transportation services provided to state enterprises and organisations of the quasi-public sector in the period from 2010 to 2017. According to the indictment, the defendants 'unjustifiably overstated the current tariffs by six to ten percent, which already included the estimated profit of the enterprise, illegally seized money.' Of course, Yerimbetov has declared the case against him to be 'politically motivated.'

Following his detention in Kazakhstan in November 2017, Yerimbetov's parents and sister claim he has been subjected to torture and his case has attracted significant international attention. On 12th, January 2018, the head of the Kazakh Office of the Ombudsman, Serik Ospanov, along with the head of the National Office for the Prevention of Torture, Igor Miroshnichenko arrived in the detention facility to visit Yerimbetov.

Acting within their remit, prosecutors opened a criminal case on the basis of allegations concerning the torture and other cruel or degrading treatment of Yerimbetov. Although forensic medical examination and fluoroscopy failed to reveal any bodily injuries, the authorities admitted a lack of full compliance with sanitary and hygienic requirements in the cells where Yerimbetov was kept. Physicians also noted that the prisoner was suffering from a 'common cold.'

In light of the continued complaints to international organisations by Yerimbetov's parents, he was subsequently visited by Ardak Zhanabilova, Chairman of the Public Monitoring Commission of Almaty, Zhemis Turmagambetova, Executive Director of the Public Foundation Charter for Human Rights, and Yevgeniy Zhovtis, Director of the Kazakhstan International Bureau for Human Rights and the Rule of Law. The visit came as a direct result of an intervention by Professor Nils Melzer, United

Nations Special Rapporteur on Torture and other Cruel, Inhuman or Degrading Treatment or Punishment, which was filed with the Government of the Republic of Kazakhstan in relation to the case. The inquiry addressed information the Special Rapporteur had received from Mr Yerimbetov's lawyer and close relatives. Whilst none of this confirmed that torture or beatings had taken place, human rights activists noted 'Yerimbetov's unhealthy appearance - he had a fever, a dry cough, and red eyes.'

Based on the results of the visit, the monitoring group recommended that given the state of Yerimbetov's health he be provided with medical assistance, including the possibility of him being placed in a ward for examination by a medical professional. 'Taking into account Mr Yerimbetov's psychological state, we recommended that he be examined by, and provided assistance from, an independent psychologist,' the experts concluded.

On February 6th, Yerimbetov was visited by Zoltan Szalai, Chargé d'affaires of the EU Delegation to Kazakhstan and diplomats from the US, the UK, Germany, France and Belgium. Shortly after, given Yerimbetov's psychological condition, at the invitation of the Prosecutor's Office, two independent British experts arrived - one a doctor specialising in forensic analysis and the other a professor of forensic psychiatry. Yerimbetov, however, refused their services, saying that he did not know them personally.

Joseph Chetrit

In 2015, Joseph Chetrit, the developer of the most expensive New York City apartment ever listed for sale, was forced to settle a lawsuit charging that he had helped launder money stolen from Kazakhstan by Mukhtar Ablyazov and Viktor Khrapunov by investing in two high-end condominium projects. BTA Bank and the City of Almaty had claimed that Chetrit conspired to hide $40 million in property deals on behalf of the pair. The money had allegedly been channelled through a shell company and invested in Chetrit's conversions of the Manhattan Flatotel and Cabrini Medical Center.

Flatotel is a former 289-room apartment style business hotel on West 52nd Street. Under the moniker 'Gramercy Square,' Cabrini's condos were to hit the market with prices ranging from $1 million to $33 million, according to the developer's filings with New York State. As part of the settlement, Chetrit and his company agreed to cooperate with the City of Almaty and BTA Bank in their claims against Ablyazov and Khrapunov. Never a part of Ablyazov's inner circle, the case against Chetrit goes to show how eager those in the world of property development are to get their hands on such substantial sums and how easy it is for the likes of Ablyazov and Khrapunov to dupe them. The outcome of the Flatotel case also proves that BTA Bank is, albeit slowly, winning the battle to recover the embezzled funds.

Given the scale of the fraud committed by Mukhtar Ablyazov and his associates and the fact that whenever or wherever matters end up in court, the judgement is always in favour of BTA Bank and the City of Almaty, it may seem incredible that the fugitive oligarch continues to enjoy support from politicians and human rights activists. How is this support achieved and maintained? With the assistance of a highly controversial human rights NGO, Ablyazov has launched something of a charm offensive in the EU.

CHAPTER EIGHT

The Fake NGO

We live in the era of 'fake news.' Whilst everyone exposed to new media tends to believe that he or she can absolutely recognise fake news for what it is, can it really be so easy? What we now refer to as fake news has been with us for a long time. Its origins include a long history of political propaganda which led us to contemporary tabloid headlines, such as the classic 'Freddie Starr Ate my Hamster' (The Sun, March 13th, 1986). There is often very little truth to be found in this genre as demonstrated by the case of the much-loved comic and the non-existent rodent. Freddie Starr was as surprised as anybody to read the unfounded allegations about him. However, fake news is not always harmful to its targets.

In Freddie Starr's case, he was to discover, almost certainly to his joy, that this spurious but very funny headline along with the accompanying text and often republished images of cuddly animals that were said to have been devoured by him between two slices of bread was to help build an urban legend. This case of fake news added to his well-deserved reputation as a hell-raiser and to his substantial fame as a top comedian and all-round entertainer. To this day, there are still people in Britain who believe that Starr made and consumed a sandwich out of a hamster known as Supersonic that belonged to the delectable Lea La Salle, a glamour model who also benefited considerably from the publicity. Such is the power of fake news.

The source of the story was the gifted publicist, Max Clifford, who numbered among his blue-chip clients' such names as Frank Sinatra and Mohammed Ali. In his day, Clifford was the unequalled master of fake news. Since Clifford was convicted of serious criminal offences of a sexual nature and sentenced to jail, where he was eventually to die in custody at the age of seventy-four, media has changed beyond recognition. The changes to the ways in which fake news is being generated now are being ruthlessly exploited by those with the need, the intellect and the financial resources to do so.

A telling contemporary example of how fake news can be disseminated through seemingly legitimate conduits is the response by the oil and gas industry to the International Panel on Climate Change (IPCC) report of 2007. Exxon Mobil, widely claimed to be among the most prolific of polluters, engaged the services of the US-based lobbying organisation, the Competitive Enterprise Institute (CEI) in order to cast doubt upon the scientific evidence of man-made (anthropogenic) climate change and global warming. In the UK, a journalist engaged by CEI as an 'associate' was tasked with producing an 'academic paper' which questioned the validity of the evidence presented by the IPCC and others.

The paper was picked up by at least one political party, the instinctively contrarian United Kingdom Independence Party (UKIP), and was to become the basis of their policy on climate change. Whilst in itself this detail of British political history may seem irrelevant, even laughable, this was the party that was subsequently held largely responsible for driving the successful campaign for the UK to withdraw from the European Union. This delivered a devastating blow to the European project, one that may prove in the medium to long term to be fatal. Such is the power of fake news.

Interestingly, CEI also represented the American tobacco giant, Philip Morris - manufacturers of Marlboro Cigarettes and other leading brands - and at least one senior member of UKIP adopted the position that passive smoking has no negative impact on public health. How enlightening it is to observe that the same people who deny climate change also defend the tobacco industry.

Mukhtar Ablyazov appears not just to have learned lessons from the CEI et al. but to have created his own model for the dissemination of such information, or rather disinformation. It is one that sanitises his past and presents him as a respectable political oppositionist, a victim of oppression and champion of human rights in the downtrodden former Soviet republics.

Mukhtar Ablyazov's Champions in the EU

The Open Dialog Foundation (ODF) was established in the Polish capital Warsaw in 2009. Initially founded by Ivan Szerstiuk, reportedly serving a sentence for ordering a murder in Ukraine, its current President is Lyudmyla Kozlovska, whose husband, Bartosz Kramek is head of the ODF Management Board. Family connections feature heavily in this saga.

According to the ODF's website, the organisation's statuary objectives include the 'protection of human rights, democracy and rule of law in the post-Soviet area.' It goes on to explain that the ODF 'pursues its goals through the organisation of observation missions, including election observation and monitoring of the human rights situation in the post-Soviet area. Based on these activities the Foundation creates its reports and distributes them among the institutions of the EU, the OSCE and other international organisations, foreign ministries and parliaments of EU countries, analytical centres and media.

'In addition to observational and analytical activities the Foundation is actively engaged in cooperation with members of parliaments involved in foreign affairs, human rights and relationships with the post-Soviet countries in order to support the process of democratisation and liberalisation of their internal policies. Significant areas of the Foundation's activities also include support programmes for political prisoners and refugees.'

There is no doubt that the post-Soviet transition towards democracy and free market economics was a time of great difficulty for many of the newly independent republics, a time of economic hardship and political and ethnic conflict. Some of the republics have still to complete that transition and continue to have residual human rights issues. Others, such as Hungary and Poland which achieved EU membership, appear now to be backsliding on basic human rights matters such as the welfare of migrants, freedom of the press and the independence of the judiciary.

The ODF, however, appears to engage in activities that go somewhat beyond their remit as outlined. A more detailed look at their statute reveals such nuggets as: 'Paragraph 8, sub-paragraph 10: Purchasing equipment, devices, materials and services, conducive to the fulfilment of the Foundation's statutory objectives, as well as providing their free of charge transfer or access to natural persons and other entities acting within the scope of the Foundation's statutory objectives.' Under the auspices of this particular clause, the ODF apparently obtained a licence from the Polish authorities that allowed them to purchase military equipment and to transfer it to the conflict zone in the Donbass Region of Eastern Ukraine.

At the beginning of August 2017, Polish Radio, Polsh reported that the authorisation had been issued by one Petr Pitel, the former head of Poland's Military Counter-Intelligence Service, whom the station claimed had been accused of cooperation with Russia's Federal Security Service. The head of the Polish Interior Ministry, Mariusz Blaschak subsequently ordered the licence to be revoked.

No less intriguing is paragraph 14, sub-paragraph 31, which allows the ODF to undertake 'Gambling and betting activities.' According to a comprehensive report on the activities and relationships of the ODF published in August 2017 by investigative reporter Marcin Rey: 'A further important source of the Foundation's funding is Bartosz Kramek and Lyudmyla Kozlovska's business entourage in Poland. Igoria Trade, the company behind an internet-based currency exchange site, deserves particular attention having donated almost half a million PLN (c. 137,000 USD). An initial investor was the Cyprus-based Banerco Ltd. a significant player in the world of online casinos and bookmakers.'

The sole director of Banerco Limited is, in fact, the corporate entity Lexact Ltd, which specialises among other things in advising clients on the gambling sector, particularly those interested in basing their business in either Cyprus or Malta. Both of these countries are major hubs for illegal online gambling enterprises and the currency exchange websites that typically operate alongside them.

Rey's detailed research revealed the identity of another major donor. The ODF, he reported, is '80 percent financed by the family and business connections of entrepreneur Petro Kozlovsky from Crimean Sevastopol, the brother of the Foundation's president, Lyudmyla Kozlovska.' Petro Kozlovsky is reported to have been involved in the supply of equipment to the Russian Navy through the company Sevastopolskiy Majak, although it has also been reported that he sold his shareholding in this company in 2003.

Polish Government Investigation into the ODF

Questions about the funding of the ODF never seem to go away. In July 2017, the Polish Ministry of Foreign Affairs (MFA) instructed the Warsaw Chamber of Tax Administration to conduct a comprehensive financial audit of the organisation. The MFA also published an open letter to the foundation in that same month, asking to see all the ODF's Management Board resolutions adopted from 2013 to the date of the letter and for an explanation as to why on its official Facebook page the foundation 'calls for illegal actions, such as encouraging people not to pay taxes.' The ministry also asked for explication as to why representatives of the ODF use social media to launch 'personal attacks on specific persons.' In his capacity as head of the ODF Management Board, Kramek also referred online to investigations by Poland's 'Social Insurance Institution (ZUS) and the National Labour Inspectorate, Państwowa Inspekcja Pracy.

In his report, Rey commented on one implausible and somewhat amusing explanation of how the foundation came by its funds. 'From its establishment in 2009 thru [sic] the end of 2016 ODF raised close to $1.8 million,' he noted. 'Foundation representatives responded to questions concerning sources of funding citing street collections and donations from prestigious entities.' As anybody who has had the experience of fund-raising in the streets will testify, it is a long and often unrewarding task. The activity can, however, act as a highly effective veil. As Kramek himself is on record as writing: 'it's impossible to identify donors who put their money in charity boxes.'

Where Does This All Lead?

A human rights NGO that supplies military equipment, including heavy machine guns, highly prized state-of-the-art FLIR thermal vision technology that can be adapted for use with sniper's rifles and which is involved with dubious gambling activities must surely arouse suspicion. There is clear evidence of government level concern about the ODF's sources of funding and the highly dubious explanation that money was raised in street collections from donors who cannot be traced.

The ODF has been involved in genuine human rights issues in the former Soviet republics, but in reality, much of this work appears to have been little more than bandwagon jumping on campaigns which already existed. In fact, the main activities of the President of the ODF, Lyudmyla Kozlovska, appear to revolve around the defence of a small number of international criminals, all of whom are extraordinarily wealthy and appear to be connected with, indeed party to, the activities of Mukhtar Ablyazov.

In addition to their work on behalf of Ablyazov, the ODF took an active role in preventing the extradition of Russian citizens Nail Malyutin and Aslan "Jako" Gagiyev from Austria to Russia. Between them, the pair stands accused of a number of extremely serious crimes, including financial fraud and masterminding the murder of business competitors. A major motivation behind the ODF's protection of Malyutin may be that his Financial Leasing Company (FLC) possibly owns, or has owned a controlling stake in Okean (Ocean) Shipyard in the city of Nikolayev, Ukraine, that in turn is a direct consumer of the production of Sevastopolskiy Majak, the company formerly owned by Peter Kozlovsky, the brother of Lyudmila Kozlovska.

Kozlovska has also been associated with the defence of both Viktor and Ilyas Khrapunov, and with Bota Jardemalie, Ablyazov's right hand during the execution of his crimes at BTA Bank. Kozlovska's name has also been linked with Olena Tyshchenko, who led investigators to Ablyazov's hideout in France and spent time in a Russian prison over allegations of money laundering relating to the period when she was acting as a legal representative to Ablyazov.

Along with her husband, Kozlovska has also been instrumental in an ongoing ODF campaign against Interpol, which led to the Red Notice against Ablyazov being removed following interventions from Members of the European Parliament at the behest of the foundation. Indeed, there have been suggestions that Ablyazov himself is the driving force behind the ODF and that he is personally funding this so-called human rights NGO. Ivan Szerstiuk, who was with the ODF from the beginning and previously led the Dialogue for Development Foundation in Lublin, where Lyudmyla Kozlovska was a co-worker, is alleged by Rey to have stated that he was receiving financial support from Ablyazov through the owner of the Ukrainian-based Fortuna Bank, Sergei Tyshchenko, the former husband of Olena Tyshchenko.

Balli Marzec, an engineer and journalist with a sound track record of promoting civil liberties, has been highly critical of both the ODF and Ablyazov, stating that 'he employs and spends big money for his lobbyists believing they will save him from fair judgement.' Marzec, who is based in Poland and campaigns for the Kazakh opposition, said on her website that 'Ablyazov calls himself an oppositionist which does huge damage to the real opposition. The real opposition in Kazakhstan has not stolen billions and does not cooperate with criminals.'

The independent Kazakhstani politician and public figure, Yermek Narymbayev is a Laureate of the Freedom Award established by the Democratic Choice of Kazakhstan (DCK) movement that Ablyazov was instrumental in founding. Under the same banner, this movement was to morph into a political party, though it failed to win a single seat in the country's parliamentary elections of 2004. Two leading members of the party, Galymzhan Zhakiyanov and Mukhtar Ablyazov have convictions for embezzlement and misuse of public office for private gain. Narymbayev, who resides in Ukraine and is personally familiar with the oligarch, has argued that the ODF was created by Ablyazov for 'protecting himself at the European Parliament.'

Another critic of Ablyazov who knows him well is Aydos Sadykov, one of the three members of the organising committee of DCK, the other two being Ablyazov and Bulat Atabaev, who reportedly lives in Germany. In July 2018, Ablyazov and Sadykov had a public spat on Facebook, the former accusing the latter of a systemic campaign to discredit the party and having him expelled from the committee. Sadykov retorted that Ablyazov had deliberately split the party, adding that 'Ablyazov is bargaining with Kazakh authorities in exchange for stopping the persecution.'

The reason for the animosity between these two former political allies appears somewhat banal: the three committee members 'theoretically enjoyed equal rights but Ablyazov cannot live that way and needs to be Number One.' For his part, Sadykov demanded the repayment of debts to journalists working for Ablyazov some years ago. It is said that any mention of Ablyazov causes great irritation to Sadykov, who refers to the runaway oligarch simply as 'a coward.'

Ablyazov Taken Off the Interpol Red List

Following an intervention led by the ODF, four Members of the European Parliament, including British Labour MEP Julie Ward signed a letter calling for the Interpol Red Notice against Ablyazov to be removed. Although they refuse to confirm or deny it as it is against their policy to discuss individual cases, this letter appears to have been instrumental in Interpol's decision.

'Being a billionaire and oligarch Mr Ablyazov is not exactly the sort of grassroots activist I am normally involved with on such cases,' Ms Ward, who had previously expressed concerns over alleged 'political abuse' of the Red Notice process, is on record as having told a member of the Brussels press corps. 'But whatever allegations he faces it is not justification for locking someone up for nothing other than politically motivated reasons. If he has done something wrong and this is proven in a court of law then he should, of course, face the consequences for any criminality.'

Ms Ward was the keynote speaker at a February 2018 conference in the European Parliament organised by the ODF and attended by Bota Jardemalie at which Mukhtar Ablyazov was discussed at length. 'I think that human rights should be at the core of our work,' she sought to confirm her credentials by telling the audience. 'All elected representatives should care about human rights… I am very busy on human rights… When I got elected, I made a decision to stand up for human rights… This is the second meeting today where I have been talking about defending human rights.'

Leaving the arena, Ward refused an approach from journalists. 'I don't deal with human rights,' she told them. 'I'm not on the human rights committee.' Closing without any opportunity whatsoever for journalists to ask questions, the "conference" was, in effect, nothing more than a lobbying event.

The ODF Campaign Against Interpol

Under the heading, 'Interpol and politically motivated extraditions,' the ODF continues to run a campaign on its website against Interpol and governments' use of the Red Notice. 'Undemocratic states are applying increasingly sophisticated methods of repression,' the organisation claims. 'They are now using the mechanisms of Interpol and international legal cooperation to persecute their opponents. Dissidents and activists who are critical of governments are the victims of the lack of control mechanisms in this area. In our reports, the Foundation monitors violations related to the abuse of the system of international police and extradition by façade democracies and authoritarian regimes. We pay special attention to the need to reform Interpol and unify the standards of protection of political refugees.'

The world's largest international police organisation with 192 member countries, the stated role of Interpol is 'to enable police around the world to work together to make the world a safer place, using a high-tech infrastructure of technical and operational support to help meet the growing challenges of fighting crime in the 21st century.'

It is interesting to note that, as is generally the case, the ODF's concerns are primarily with the well-being of the mega-rich, either wanted or convicted, whose human rights they represent. It is reasonable to wonder whether they believe Ablyazov, the Khrapunovs or Jardemalie to be innocent political dissidents and not criminals.

Criticism of the ODF in the European Parliament

Centre-Right MEP, Anna Fotyga, former Minister of Foreign Affairs in Poland and Chair of the European Parliament's Subcommittee on Security and Defence worked closely with the ODF for a period of time, particularly on issues relating to Ukraine and Moldova. She has now 'totally severed' her connection with the foundation because she says, it has 'ceased to be a non-political NGO and is not a credible organisation.'

Fotyga said she had reacted with 'disgust at the scandalous text' posted on social media by Bartosz Kramek of the ODF with regards to Poland under the headline: 'Let the State Come to a Stop: Let's Shut Down the Government!' The message, said the MEP, was 'promoted by the foundation itself,' further stating that 'calls for destabilisation of the state clearly indicate that the ODF has ceased to be a non-political NGO and has nothing to do with its name.'

'Regardless of motivation - whether it is a search for funds for further activity or the desire for political self-determination - this is a conscious choice,' Fotyga stated, a move which overshadowed the ODF's previous achievements and 'shows the immaturity of its leadership... In fulfilling the mandate as an MEP I always broadly try to build support for relevant issues on the EU's Eastern policy. Several broad initiatives have been supported by ODF but I can give an assurance that all events and initiatives in which ODF will be involved will be met with a boycott [by me] and I would encourage the same action by colleagues from all political groups and international partners.'

They Are Going to Put You in the Movies

It was a special moment when, in June 2018, the press corps in Brussels unexpectedly received in their in-boxes a mass email of a video purporting to show ODF President Lyudmyla Kozlovska in flagrante delicto with none other than Mukhtar Ablyazov. In the press rooms of the European institutions, there was only one topic of conversation for an hour or so that morning.

The lady in question issued an online denial on June 20th, 2018 which dominated the ODF website. 'Please be advised that any video recordings recently posted on the Internet allegedly involving Lyudmyla Kozlovska, associating her with Bill Browder, initiator of the Global Magnitsky Law campaign, and Mukhtar Ablyazov, leader of the opposition movement "Democratic Choice of Kazakhstan", are fake,' it stated. In the immortal words of William Shakespeare, 'The Lady Doth Protest Too Much, Methinks.'

Two versions of the video were posted online, one on YouTube and the other - far more explicit - appeared on a hard-core pornographic website. It must be said that the latter was somewhat amateurish in that the action took place on a side of the bed that was out of camera shot. It was a mistake that professional security services would never have made, leading some to suggest that Kozlovska may herself have been behind the production for whatever reason motivates such people. It is certainly the case that Ablyazov if it is indeed him, displays his genitals to the camera, whilst Kozlovska's modesty - if it is indeed her - is carefully preserved. To the credit of the press corps, the more explicit video was not discussed, at least not outside the bars and restaurants of the European Quarter.

Just weeks later, another video appeared after a young Ukrainian journalist, Lilya Tkachuk door-stepped Kozlovska in Brussels. The eminent human rights campaigner just happened to be in the company of Bota Jardemalie, looking resplendent with her Chanel handbag. Such are the deprived lives that political refugees lead. Refusing to answer any questions, Kozlovska and Jardemalie instead acted petulantly, photographing Tkachuk and calling the police to the scene to confirm her journalistic credentials.

Kozlovska's Removal from Belgium

On Saturday 18th, August 2018, it was reported by Politico, a US-based news organisation that has a significant presence in Brussels, that Lyudmyla Kozlovska, having flown into Brussels from Kyiv earlier in the week, had found herself flagged in the Schengen Information System (SIS) as a person of danger to Polish national security. As previously mentioned, Kozlovska and her Polish husband Bartosz Kramek have led several campaigns against the Polish Government, including one apparently urging citizens to withhold taxes. Belgian authorities confirmed that she was stopped late on the night of Monday 13th and was sent back to Kyiv the following morning.

The Polish Government declined to discuss the matter with Politico at the time. The Polish Security Service, however, stated that they had 'issued a negative opinion regarding' an application for a long-term residency permit from Kozlovska. 'As a result, Mrs Kozlovska has been banned from entering the territory of Poland and the EU,' Stanisław Żaryn, a spokesman for the head of Poland's Security Service, said in a statement. This 'negative opinion' issued by the Counterintelligence Department of Poland's Internal Security Agency (ABW) stemmed from 'serious doubts regarding the funding of the Open Dialog Foundation Kozlovska is running, which may produce further legal effects... Given the statutory constraints as well as the ongoing tax inspection, for the time being no further details of this matter can be made available to the public.'

Giving her side of the story, Kozlovska stated: 'I was asked by the border police officer of the Brussels Airport what kind of crime I did in Poland. I said I didn't do anything. But they said, "Poland is looking for you on a high alert. There is a ban to enter the Schengen countries." I told the police officer that I recognise the case as one of political prosecution of my husband and Polish authorities want to punish him.'

The image, taken from a mildly pornographic video clip distributed to the Brussels press corp in June 2018 purports to show ODF President Lyudmyla Kozlovska 'in flagrante delicto' with Mukhtar Ablyazov.

As is the case with the clients of the ODF, the line of defence arguing that any case is a matter of 'political persecution' was somewhat predictable. One might ask of Kozlovska, who has Polish residency, as well as Ukrainian and, reportedly, a Russian passport - although she has appeared somewhat reticent to admit to the latter which may or may not have been bestowed upon her by the Putin regime following the illegal annexation of Crimea - if it has ever occurred to her to ask how her 'politically persecuted' clients earned their billions?

Under the auspices of the Organisation for Security and Cooperation in Europe (OSCE), the Human Dimension Implementation Meeting Conference 2018 was held in Warsaw from the 10th -21st September. During a discussion involving delegates from Armenia, Italy, Lithuania, Ukraine and the UK focussing on the important and highly relevant topic of 'Cooperation between Government and Civil Society in Post-Soviet Countries,' serious concerns were raised about the growing use of 'fake news' by NGOs in the pursuit of dubious agendas.

Evidence of the manipulation of political party manifestos and of coercion of individual politicians at European level was discussed at the conference, and, almost inevitably in such a context, the locally based ODF dominated the debate. The conference considered suspicions that the ODF has received significant funding from Ablyazov and that members of the European Parliament have been subverted by an ODF campaign that benefited the fugitive after several MEPs signed a letter which called for the Interpol Red Notice against him to be lifted. 'This is a subversion of the European Parliament and an undermining of the power of a law enforcement agency which protects the security of millions of European citizens,' a delegate from the UK stated.

The charges against Ablyazov were discussed in some detail. Others facing similar charges and associated with Ablyazov were also named during the conference, including Viktor and Ilyas Khrapunov, Bota Jardemalie, Askar Kupesov and Nail Malyutin. 'How strange it is that all the so-called political dissidents that ODF represent seem to have convictions for money laundering, and that ODF itself has received funding from online gambling companies,' it was noted.

It was also remarked upon that in 2016 the ODF had lobbied not only the European Parliament but also the Parliamentary Assembly of the Council of Europe (PACE) regarding the case of one Vyacheslav Platon Kobalyev, a Moldovan citizen, reputedly one the country's richest men. He is currently serving an 18-year prison sentence having been found guilty of fraud and money laundering. A declaration by PACE (No. 617, 11th, October 2016) calling for Kobalyev's release describes him as having been subjected to 'political persecution.' Could this be a coincidence? Highly unlikely, one might think.

Following the Warsaw conference, delegates unanimously signed a written declaration stating that 'foundations such as the Open Dialog use the money of their sponsors and distort real information about the human rights situation and try to propagandise [their] biased point of view in countries with a developing civil society. In this regard, constructive cooperation between government and the non-governmental sector can be threatened.' Delegates called on the OSCE leadership to 'pay attention to the activities of the Open Dialog Foundation, which has an ambiguous reputation in the countries of the European Union.'

At this point, one might be forgiven for considering Mukhtar Ablyazov as something of a lovable rogue. He is certainly gifted with financial acumen. He also has a certain charm with the ladies, especially blonde ones who are married to somebody else. It should be noted, however, that all those he comes into contact with find their lives seriously tainted by the experience. Now, after a recent jail cell confession from a convicted killer, we may start to look upon the fugitive oligarch in an altogether different light.

Yerzhan Nureldaemovich Tatishev
(1967-2004) Ablyazov's predecessor
as head of the BTA Bank

CHAPTER NINE

Murder Most Foul

The shooting 'accident' that took the life of Yerzhan Tatishev, then head of Kazakhstan's BTA Bank, by a single rifle shot to the head whilst driving a car on a hunting expedition, has since been proven to be an act of murder, and one that certainly benefitted Mukhtar Ablyazov considerably. At the wheel of a Toyota Land Cruiser, Tatishev was chasing wolves across the steppe along with two fellow hunters. After catching up with the animals, he handed his rifle to Muratkhan Tokmadi, who was sitting in the back seat. Tokmadi is widely alleged to have been a key player in an organised crime group known as the Deputatsky Korpus (Corps of Deputies), whose members terrorised the business community in the late 1990s and early 2000s.

According to the experts' conclusions at that time, the vehicle unexpectedly hit a bump on the road causing the gun to discharge by accident. The bullet hit the banker in the occipital part of his head and exited his skull through the left eye. At the time of his death, the 38-year-old Tatishev owned 24 percent of the voting shares of BTA Bank.

An official report on the incident by US State Department officials later made public on WikiLeaks concluded that: 'the fate of BTA and of Tatishev's 24 percent share will, most likely, prove the best explanation of his untimely death.' As the man responsible for Tatishev's death, Muratkhan Tokmadi received a one-year jail sentence for causing 'death through negligence.'

Tokmadi's Jail Cell Confession

The story was to take an unexpectedly dramatic twist. Following technical investigations into the weapon involved carried out by experts from the US together with witness testimonies, Tokmadi was to make a dramatic jail cell confession. He described how the shooting was no mere accident but effectively a contract killing ordered by the man who was then to take over the bank, Mukhtar Ablyazov. Tokmadi related how during several meetings the pair discussed 'the elimination of Yerzhan' and how, as he claimed, Ablyazov persuaded him to carry out the murder and discussed how to make it 'look like an accidental killing.'

Appearing in front of the Kazakh Judge, Azamat Tlepov, he admitted his guilt, telling the court that in 2004 he was under pressure from Ablyazov, who threatened to kill him and his family if he did not murder Tatishev. Tokmadi also confessed to bribing a senior official to falsify evidence in order to support the claim that the shooting was accidental.

'The criminal case was transferred for investigation to the investigative and operational group of the Ministry of Internal Affairs of the Republic of Kazakhstan, headed by Yerzhan Artykbaev,' Tokmadi said. 'I tried to persuade him to show loyalty to me; not to apply to me the preventive measure in the form of arrest and further assist in the investigation. I handed Artykbaev money in an envelope in the amount of, as I recall, 20,000 US dollars. He put it in his portfolio and said, time will tell.

'I tried to change the conclusions of the examination, and I was looking for the possibility to meet with the experts. I then met with a private expert. In his office, I gave him the money in the amount of 20,000 US dollars. As a result, it was concluded that the gun could fire spontaneously,' Tokmadi added. 'After that, there were investigative measures and courts for three years. And everything ended loyally - causing death by negligence.'

Tokmadi's Conviction for Murder

Following the confession, a trial was held in the Zhambyl Region's specialised inter-district criminal court that lasted a month and heard testimony from more than fifty witnesses. These included US forensics experts, who revealed how the murder weapon was subtly altered whilst in police custody to make it look as though it was faulty at the time of Tatishev's death. The US experts also presented the results of blood spatter analysis that confirmed the shot could have only have been made deliberately from the rear seat of the car in which Tokmadi was sitting. On March 16th, 2018, Tokmadi was sentenced to ten-and-a-half years in a maximum-security prison, although the prosecution had argued for a twelve-year sentence. At the time of the trial, Tokmadi was already serving a three-year prison term on an extortion and possession of illegal firearms conviction.

In a somewhat dramatic twist to proceedings, a few days before the trial came to its conclusion, on the evening of March 8th, Tokmadi managed to stage an escape from a prison hospital. All roads surrounding Taraz, in the south of Kazakhstan near the Kyrgyz border, were blocked by the Kazakh police, who recaptured him in a matter of hours, according to local media reports.

Following the confession and conviction of Tokmadi, in addition to numerous fraud allegations around the world, an outstanding twenty-two-month sentence for contempt of court in the UK and another of twenty-years in his home country, Mukhtar Ablyazov is now the subject of a murder investigation.

The family of Yerzhan Tatishev issued the following statement: 'Yerzhan lives in our hearts. Today, when the truth has finally emerged, and the killer has pleaded guilty, we want to say thank you to people who, like us, believed in justice and supported us in this struggle. This struggle lasted fourteen years, but justice has triumphed over time.

'It was hard for us. It was hard and painful when monstrous crimes were hidden behind power and money, and behind politics. But there were always people who, like us, believed in the power of the law and fought for the truth. And the legal punishment that occurred was within the framework of an honest investigation and an open and fair trial. No-one should escape punishment for their evil deeds. Today, after many years, we know and believe that all persons involved in the crimes against Yerzhan will be punished. Without exception.

'This faith will not return our son, brother, husband, and father to us, but a sense of justice gives us strength to live with the pain of loss. We want to appeal to all people who are looking for justice today. Do not stop. Carry your point. Fight for justice even when no one believes you. This is the only thing worth fighting for.'

Dramatic reconstruction of the moment when Muratkhan Tokmadi, by his own admission, murdered Yerzhan Tatishev with a shot to the head

CHAPTER TEN

Europe Welcomes 'Stolen' Billions

The sheer scale of the fraud and corruption, not to mention other serious crimes committed by Mukhtar Ablyazov and his cronies may seem astonishing but they are, in fact, the mere tip of the iceberg. Europe has become a haven for such people.

Why is it that national authorities' have allowed people who are subject to international arrest warrants and, in some cases, multiple extradition requests to remain at large? People who, as in the case of Ablyazov, have even committed offences and received jail sentences in EU member states? Despite their transgressions, their lack of respect for the laws of the countries that have granted them asylum and the multiple outstanding extradition orders against them, they are allowed not only to remain at large but even enjoy enhanced security at the taxpayers' expense.

Could this have anything to do with the billions they bring with them, or could it be the high-level contacts they enjoy? Rumours about connections with prominent European and US businessmen and even royalty abound. Or could it, as in the case of the UK, have anything to do with the fact that vast sums of dirty money are laundered through property purchases? In 2017, Transparency International UK identified London properties worth a total of £4.2 billion ($5.8 billion) that were bought by individuals with suspicious wealth.

The properties in question are often left uninhabited in for many years - and London is, of course, a city with an increasing problem with homelessness. This phenomenon also has the effect of keeping land and property prices in London artificially inflated, generating significant wealth for the major property owners in the city, some of whom are amongst the most powerful individuals and institutions in the country. Would the net beneficiaries of such a situation have any interest in changing it?

Unexplained Wealth Orders

The UK has recently introduced new Unexplained Wealth Orders (UWOs), which are to be used to seize the UK assets of oligarchs and others suspected of having profited from the proceeds of crime. The orders were introduced in the Criminal Finance Act in 2017 but only began to come into effect in January 2018. The provision has been nicknamed the "McMafia law" after the BBC's true-story drama based on money laundering and international organised crime.

The first such order was imposed on February 28th, 2018 on an unnamed politician from Central Asia with a multi-million-pound property portfolio. As the subject ignored the order against them, the National Crime Agency (NCA) was granted by the courts the power to enforce a UWO worth £22m ($30 million) and to freeze their assets. The orders related to two properties, one in London and one in the South-East of England.

'Unexplained Wealth Orders have the potential to significantly reduce the appeal of the UK as a destination for illicit income,' said Donald Toon, the NCA's head of economic crime. 'They enable the UK to more effectively target the problem of money laundering through prime real estate in London and elsewhere.'

The wife of the politician, known only as Mrs A, went back to court in July 2018 in an attempt to overturn the order. During her appeal, further details of the lifestyle the couple enjoyed were revealed, including the fact that over an undisclosed period during ten years, she had spent no less than £16 million at Harrods. Intriguingly, it was also revealed that Mr A is a former banker who has spent time in jail abroad as a result of a large-scale fraud investigation. During his defence, the accused's counsel, James Lewis QC appeared to imply that Mr A was the victim of some form of political persecution. 'It seemed the whole case was being decided against him by the presidential administration. This was a Kafkaesque trial,' the Sunday Times reported him saying on July 26th, 2018.

These words are, of course, highly reminiscent of the ODF's defence of Mukhtar Ablyazov. The similarities between the two cases as well as those involving the Khrapunov family are striking. It would appear that these international rogues hit upon a successful formula for laundering money and then use the legal system in their country of refuge in order to obtain protection by pleading 'political persecution.'

What one might merely dismiss as a series of coincidences, in fact, suggests that Ablyazov et al. have found a formula that appears to work rather well. Get out-of-town fast, invest your ill-gotten gains in property, ideally through shell companies; make friends in high places, position yourself as a political refugee and then play the system. Not usually a man prone to making mistakes, Ablyazov failed to play the system well enough, leading to his ignominious flight from English justice on a bus, leaving tens of millions behind.

Tax Havens and Loopholes

The EU has slowly been stepping up its pressure on tax havens. Although there has long been an interest in this issue, however, there remains strong opposition from certain member states such as the UK, which, perhaps quite correctly, perceives the attention being focussed on the Channel Islands as motivated by the French desire to eventually wrest control of the Islands from Great Britain. The islands are not members of the EU, nor do they express any desire to become so. Indeed, EU membership is the last thing they appear to want. Brexit should guarantee their economic status. Being British Crown Dependencies has always led to a degree of vulnerability and uncertainty in respect to UK membership of the EU.

Luxembourg, which is the EU's wealthiest tax haven and has absolutely no desire whatsoever to change this situation, has managed to avoid the spotlight in this debate by virtue of being a full EU Member. Owing to the requirement for unanimity in the European Council, the tiny Duchy can rest assured that if it were to come to the worst, it could veto any proposal for sanctions against it. With a population of 602,000, Luxembourg has virtually no industry as such beyond moving money around and hosting "secret" bank accounts. In March 2010, the Sunday Telegraph reported that most of Kim Jong-il's $4 billion in secret accounts are stashed away in Luxembourg's banks.

According to World Bank and International Monetary Fund figures from 2017, Luxembourg enjoys the highest Gross Domestic Product (GDP) in Europe and the third highest in the world. In order to attract investment into the country, tax loopholes abound. The Tax Justice Network's Financial Secrecy Index (2013) ranked Luxembourg as the second most obscure financial centre in the world behind Switzerland and just ahead of the Cayman Islands, Hong Kong and Singapore. The TJN report described Luxembourg the '"Death Star" of financial secrecy.'

In October 2017, Amazon was ordered to pay about 250 million euros ($295 million) in back-taxes to Luxembourg, a fine much lower than some sources close to the case had expected and just a fraction of the €13 billion that Apple Inc. was ordered to pay to Ireland the previous year. EU Competition Commissioner, Margrethe Vestager, who oversaw both cases, said at the time that 'Luxembourg gave illegal tax benefits to Amazon. As a result, almost three quarters of Amazon's profits were not taxed.'

In a press statement issued in June 2018, the European Commission announced that it had found that Luxembourg allowed two French corporate groups to avoid paying taxes on almost all their profits for about a decade without any valid justification. This is illegal under EU State Aid rules because it gave the French energy groups an undue advantage. Luxembourg was obliged to recover about €120 million in unpaid taxes.

The man at the helm of the Government of Luxembourg during the period covered by these controversial episodes was the current President of the European Commission, Jean Claude Juncker. As well as being Prime Minister (1995-2013), he also juggled the roles of Minister for Finances (1989-2009) and Minister for the Treasury (2009-2013). With those three portfolios under his belt, he would have had an enormous degree of control over financial dealings within the little tax haven.

In an interview with the Luxembourg newspaper d'Lëtzebuerger Land in 2003, the former head of tax affairs for Amazon, Bob Comfort said that the 'Luxembourg Government presents itself as a business partner, and I think it's an accurate description: it helps to solve problems.' Of Juncker, who at the time of Amazon's negotiations with Luxembourg was serving as both prime minister and finance minister, Comfort added that 'his message was simple: "If you encounter problems which you don't seem to be able to resolve, please come back and tell me. I'll try to help."' Shortly before he retired in 2014, Comfort was appointed as Luxembourg's Honorary Consul for the Seattle Region. An official announcement noted that he enjoyed 'a long-standing relationship with Luxembourg.'

Although Juncker went on to become President of the European Commission, many of the complex tax deals that took place on his watch are still being unravelled. All this seems unbelievable, but then Switzerland, home to the Khrapunov family and their considerable wealth, comes out even worse than Luxembourg on the Tax Justice Network's Financial Secrecy Index. Is it any wonder that such an environment would prove so attractive to fraudsters?

Ablyazov, seen here drinking
with friends in his private jet, enjoyed the high life.

CHAPTER ELEVEN

The Threat to Democracy

The story of Mukhtar Ablyazov and his network is an understated sensation. It is also an indictment of the Western financial system. Vast sums have circulated through banks that have not been held to account. Companies have been set up across frontiers in order to embezzle and legitimise fraudulently obtained funds. The political establishment has been drawn into criminal conspiracies. Politicians have become embroiled, and a few of them have been held to account. Governments have benefitted from enormous transfers that have enabled Ablyazov and his associates to escape justice, and still, the saga continues.

In late 2017, the collective eyebrows of the Brussels press corps were raised in unison as a rumour began to circulate that Ablyazov had struck a deal with the Belgian Government for citizenship, immunity and safe haven from the authorities of Russia, Ukraine, the UK and Kazakhstan in return for providing evidence in the Belgian 'Kazakhgate' scandal. Sources claimed that Ablyazov had held a series of secret talks during the summer of that year with Dirk Van der Maelen, the President of the Belgian Kazakhgate commission.

In May 2018, the lawyer and former Belgian minister, Armand De Decker was indicted for influence-peddling as part of the wide-ranging probe into allegations of corruption. This was the first time the Belgian authorities had charged anyone in connection with a case which had already led to proceedings against several people in the UK and France and raids on the offices of the European aviation giant, Airbus.

De Decker was one of the lawyers for Uzbek businessman, Patokh Chodiev, part-owner of the Eurasian Resources Group (ERG), estimated by Forbes to be worth between $2-3 billion. With his partners, Alexander Mashkevich and Alijan Ibragimov - both also billionaires implicated in the Kazakhgate scandal - Chodiev had built a metals and mining empire in Kazakhstan.

Interestingly, on June 27th, 1997, Chodiev acquired Belgian citizenship. This led to a debate in the media about how his naturalisation was obtained, since Chodiev does not speak any of the three official languages of Belgium - French, Flemish or German - fluently, this being a prerequisite for obtaining a Belgian passport. Furthermore, the Belgian State Security Service had expressed its concerns about Chodiev's relationships with certain Russian businessmen. Chodiev found himself accused of having received help in this matter from the mayor of the historically famous Belgian town of Waterloo, Serge Kubla. In 2007, the Belgian newspaper La Dernière Heure reported that Chodiev was himself a resident of Waterloo.

Chodiev's naturalisation was to become the subject of an official inquiry, about which the Belgian newspaper, Le Soir reported on 11th, January 2017. 'When Serge Kubla wrote to Claude Eerdekens on 16th, May 1997,' the piece states, 'all the lights were already green for Chodiev: he had the support of the SPF Justice, the State Security Service, the Aliens Department, the Waterloo police and the Public Prosecutor's Office, and therefore also that of the naturalisation service.'

According to a statement from the Prosecutor's Office in Mons, the 2018 indictment of De Decker saw the former Belgian Development

Cooperation Minister suspected of having sought 'to facilitate the gran-ting of a transactional procedure' in favour of Chodiev. A magistrate 'sent a letter notifying him of his indictment for influence peddling,' adding that the alleged events took place in 2011. At that time, De Decker had just joined the team in charge of defending oligarchs including Chodiev in a corruption case in Belgium.

Also a former Vice President of the Belgian Senate, De Decker alle-gedly used his influence to obtain a meeting at the home of then Justice Minister, Stefaan De Clerck to plead his client's cause. De Decker, who denied influence-peddling, resigned from Belgian Prime Minister Charles Michel's liberal Reform Movement (MR), on Monday, May 7th, 2018. In June 2011, Chodiev and his two co-defendants had avoided trial by paying a hefty settlement reported as being 522,500 euros ($640,000).

This was possible under Belgian law because of the unreasonable length of the judicial inquiry, which was still not concluded after 15 years, and so, the three men left court on February 18th, 2011 safe in the knowledge that they would not face jail. As a result of this settlement, it should be emphasised that no judgement was made against Chodiev, Mashkevich and Ibragimov in this matter and they are therefore presu-med innocent. In April 2016, Chodiev was named among the 732 Bel-gians linked to offshore companies when the Panama Papers scandal hit the headlines.

What Ablyazov could have added to a legal case that is now closed is a matter of speculation, but certainly, the behaviour of the Kazakhgate commission has come in for heavy criticism. Belgium, like its Benelux neighbour, the tax haven Luxembourg, is well known for its political corruption, political and economic patronage and nepotism. A relatively small country with a correspondingly small economy, Belgium has a bloated and highly pampered public sector and a hugely expensive and highly secretive monarchy. It also has a frighteningly vast government debt of 103.1 percent of Gross Domestic Product (Eurostat 2017). Such an environment is perfect for the likes of Ablyazov.

Another person to have found sanctuary in Belgium as a political refugee is Bota Jardemalie, Ablyazov's former 'right hand' at BTA Bank and his alleged former mistress. Both are, of course, represented by the same controversial so-called human rights NGO, the Open Dialog Foundation.

Throughout this story, not one of the characters presented could conceivably be considered to be 'normal.' Surely, not even the ODF could stretch the boundaries of 'coincidence' so far while keeping a straight face. But the story may well not end there. Cases in which Ablyazov is implicated are ongoing in the US, and although France does not have an extradition treaty with Kazakhstan, it does have such an arrangement with Russia and Ukraine. In spite of France's previous refusal to enact these extradition requests, that these arrangements remain live leaves Ablyazov vulnerable, especially whilst legal actions in France continue against him. The final chapter of what may be described as one of the greatest financial and political scandals of our time has yet to be seen.

APPENDICES

1. HIGH COURT OF JUSTICE, 23rd Nov 2012,
Judgment entered in favour of BTA Bank

2. EASTERN CARIBBEAN SUPREME COURT,
May 2013, application made by Mukhtar Ablyazov to set aside
the registration of two judgments entered against him in the
Commercial Court in England in favour of the Respondent JSC
BTA Bank fails

3. PRESS RELEASE, 22nd Oct 2015,
Hogan Lovells Secures Success in UK Supreme Court for BTA Bank
in Ablyazov Fraud Case

4. SUPREME COURT PRESS SUMMARY, 21st MARCH 2018,
BTA Bank (Respondent) v Khrapunov (Appellant)

5. HIGH COURT OF JUSTICE, 21st June 2018,
Approval of judgement against Mukhtar Ablyazov and Ilyas
Khrapunov

6. LAW SOCIETY GAZETTE, 29th AUG 2018,
High Court: 'no merit' to Kazakh's extradition fears in £4.6bn fraud
hearing

7. POLISH MINISTRY OF FOREIGN AFFAIRS,
News release concerning letter to Open Dialog Foundation

IN THE HIGH COURT OF JUSTICE   Claim No. 2011 FOLIO 79
QUEEN'S BENCH DIVISION
COMMERCIAL COURT

Before the Honourable Mr Justice Teare
Dated 23 November 2012

BETWEEN:

JSC BTA BANK

Claimant/Applicant

and

MUKHTAR ABLYAZOV

Defendant/Respondent

ORDER

UPON THE APPLICATION of the Applicant ("the Bank") by application notice dated 19 November 2012 (the "Application")

AND UPON READING the order made by Mr Justice Teare dated 29 February 2012 (the "Debarring Order"), the order made by Lords Justice Maurice Kay, Rix and Toulson dated 7 November 2012, and the order made by Mr Justice Teare dated 9 November 2012

AND UPON the First Defendant ("Mr Ablyazov") being debarred from further defending this action and the Bank being at liberty to enter judgment against him under paragraph 3 of the Debarring Order

AND UPON READING the evidence filed

AND UPON HEARING Counsel for the Bank and Counsel for Mr Ablyazov

IT IS ORDERED THAT:

1   The stay imposed by the Order of Mr Justice Teare made by consent on 8 November 2011 be lifted as against Mr Ablyazov.

2   Judgment is entered in favour of the Bank in the amounts of:

     (a)   £1,021,591,758.13 pursuant to the Amended Claim Form issued on 25 January 2011;

(b) £23,915,802.49 interest accrued from the date of the amended claim form to the date of this Order at a rate of 1.5% per annum;

(c) £229,152.34 per day continuing interest accruing at the judgment rate of 8% per annum from the date of this Order until payment.

3 Mr Ablyazov do pay the Claimant's costs of the claim as against Mr Ablyazov (including the costs of the Application) on the standard basis to be the subject of detailed assessment if not agreed.

4 Mr Ablyazov do pay to the Bank by 4pm on 7 December 2012 the sums in paragraph 2 above.

<u>IN THE HIGH COURT OF JUSTICE</u>

Claim No: 2011 Folio 79

QUEEN'S BENCH DIVISION
COMMERCIAL COURT
Before the Honourable Mr Justice Teare
Dated 23 November 2012
B E T W E E N:

JSC BTA BANK

<u>Claimant/Applicant</u>

- and -

MUKHTAR ABLYAZOV

<u>Defendant/Respondent</u>

ORDER

Solicitors for the Claimant:
Hogan Lovells International LLP
Atlantic House,
Holborn Viaduct,
London
EC1A 2FG

Tel: 020 7296 2000
Fax: 020 7296 2001
DX: London/Chancery Lane 57

May 2013 application made by Mukhtar Ablyazov ('to set aside the registration of two judgments entered against him in the Commercial Court in England in favour of the Respondent JSC BTA Bank fails.

IN THE EASTERN CARIBBEAN SUPREME COURT
IN THE HIGH COURT OF JUSTICE
VIRGIN ISLANDS
COMMERCIAL DIVISION

CLAIM NO: BVIHC (COM) 0125/2012

In the matter of
   Section 3 of The Reciprocal Enforcement Of Judgments Act (CAP.65)
And in the matter of
   An application to register a judgment of the High Court of Justice in England
Between:

JSC BTA BANK

Respondent

and

MUKHTAR ABLYAZOV

Applicant

Appearances: Mr George Hayman and Mr Robert Nader for the Applicant, Mukhtar Ablyazov
Mr Philip Jones QC, Mr Mark Forte and Ms Tameka Davis for the Respondent, JSC BTA Bank

2013: 25 April, 2 May

JUDGMENT

(Reciprocal Enforcement of Judgments Act, 1922 ('the Act') – application to set aside order for registration of English judgments on the grounds that they are under appeal – whether proposed application to European Court of Human Rights ('ECtHR') is an appeal for the purposes of subsection 3(2)(e) of the Act – whether real prospect that ECtHR may declare against the English judgments such that the English Courts may reopen them and possibly set them aside – whether unjust or inconvenient that the English judgments should be registered in the Territory until outcome and effect of application to ECtHR known – meaning and effect of subsection 3(1) of the Act considered – whether contrary to public policy to permit registration and enforcement prior to that)

[1] This is an application made by Mukhtar Ablyazov ('Mr Ablyazov') to set aside the registration here in the High Court of two judgments entered against him in the Commercial Court in England in favour of the Respondent JSC BTA Bank ('the Bank') on 23 November 2012 ('the English judgments'). The English judgments are for the payment of money and together make Mr Ablyazov liable to the Bank for in excess of USD 2 billion. The order for registration was made on 13 December 2012, but was not to take effect until after Mr Ablyazov's application to the United Kingdom Supreme Court for permission to appeal to that Court against the dismissal by the English Court of Appeal of his appeals against the unless orders made by Teare J on 29 February 2012 ('the unless orders') was refused, or if granted, until his subsequent appeal was dismissed. The Supreme Court refused Mr Ablyazov permission to appeal on 21 February 2013, so that the registrations in the High Court here took effect upon the same day, but subject to any application by Mr Ablyazov to have them set aside..

[2] The English judgments were entered as a result of alleged non-compliance by Mr Ablyazov with disclosure orders included in world wide freezing orders which had been made against him in the course of the English proceedings. I say 'alleged' not because I have any view as to whether Mr Ablyazov has complied, but simply to indicate that his non compliance is not a fact found by me on any of these applications. As a result, Mr Ablyazov had been sentenced to twenty two months imprisonment for contempt of Court. He had not, however, surrendered to the relevant authority and by 29 February 2012, when Teare J made the unless orders, had, to all intents and purposes, disappeared.

[3] It was against this background that on 29 February 2012 Teare J ordered (1) that Mr Ablyazov surrender to the authorities so that he could be delivered to prison; (2) that he repeat the exercise of disclosing his world wide assets; and (3) that if he had not done those things by 4 pm on 9 and 14 March 2012 respectively, he should be debarred from defending the proceedings and the Bank would be at liberty to enter judgment against him. It was for failure to comply with either order that his defences were struck out and judgment was entered against him, as I have said, on 23 November 2012.

[4] Mr Ablyazov appealed the making of the unless orders to the English Court of Appeal. The judgments themselves were not appealed, the view being taken, no doubt correctly, that until the unless orders were set aside, the judgments were regular and unimpeachable. After a three day hearing in July 2012 the Court of Appeal dismissed Mr Ablyazov's appeal on 6 November 2012. The only point which I need to mention is that Toulson LJ (as he then was) dissented as to the propriety of making Mr Ablyazov's defence of the proceedings conditional upon his surrender to the authorities, which he considered to be in the nature of a double punishment. But as Toulson LJ pointed out and as Mr Philip Jones QC, who appeared, together with Mr Mark Forte and Ms Tameka Davis, for the Respondent Bank on these applications stressed, the point was academic, since all three judges in any event agreed that Mr Ablyazov should have been debarred

from defending for non-disclosure. As I have said, the United Kingdom Supreme Court refused permission to appeal from that decision, the ground given being that the proposed appeal did not raise a point of law of general public importance which required consideration by the Supreme Court at that time.

[5]   Mr Ablyazov has thus run out of avenues in the English Courts, but he intends to apply to the European Court of Human Rights (the ECtHR') for a declaration that the striking out of his defences amounted to a violation of his Article 6 rights (to a court and to a fair hearing) and that execution of the judgments would infringe his right to property under Article 1 of the European Convention on Human Rights ('the ECHR'). Indeed, on 22 April 2013 his Solicitors submitted a Letter of Introduction to the Registrar of the ECtHR indicating that intention. I assume for the purposes of this application that the applications to the ECtHR will be made in due course and will be prosecuted to the point of determination.

The argument for Mr Ablyazov on these applications

[6]   Before turning to Mr Ablyazov's submissions on these applications it is necessary to set out the relevant provisions of the Act:

  (1) '(1) Where a judgment has been obtained in the High Court in England or in Northern Ireland or in the Court of Session in Scotland the judgment creditor may apply to the High Court at any time within twelve months after the date of the judgment or such longer period as may be allowed by the Court to have the judgment registered in the High Court and on any such application the Court may, if in all the circumstances of the case they think it is just and convenient that the judgment should be enforced in the Territory, and subject to the provisions of this section, order the judgment to be registered accordingly.'

  (2) No judgment shall be ordered to be registered under this section if-

   (a) the original Court acted without jurisdiction; or

   (b) the judgment debtor, being a person who was neither carrying on business nor ordinarily resident within the jurisdiction of the original Court, did not voluntarily appear otherwise submit or agree to submit to the jurisdiction of that Court; or

   (c) the judgment debtor being the defendant in the proceedings, was not duly served with the process of the original Court and did not appear, notwithstanding that he was ordinarily resident or was carrying business within the jurisdiction of that Court or agreed to submit to the jurisdiction of that Court; or

   (d) the judgment was obtained by fraud; or

    (e) the judgment debtor satisfies the High Court either than an appeal is pending, or that he is entitled and intends to appeal, against the judgment; or

    (f) the judgment was in respect of a cause of action which for reasons of public policy or for some other similar reason could not have been entertained by the High Court.

[7] Mr George Hayman, who has appeared, together with Mr Robert Nader, for Mr Ablyazov, submits that the BVI judgments[1] should be set aside on two grounds. First, he submits that Mr Ablyazov's intended application to the ECtHR is an appeal for the purposes of section 3(2)(e) of the Act. That submission is unsustainable. An appeal is a proceeding whose outcome, if successful, will result in the making of an order, binding on the Court whose judgment or order is being appealed, setting aside or varying the judgment or order appealed from. Mr Hayman does not and cannot suggest that the ECtHR has the power to set aside or vary the judgment of the English Court of Appeal. For the same reasons, the proposed application cannot be treated as if it were an appeal, since it has none of the characteristics of an appeal. It is in the nature of a complaint against the Government of the United Kingdom.

[8] Mr Hayman's second submission is more formidable. He submits that because the processes of the ECtHR may result in a recommendation or declaration which may enable Mr Ablyazov to persuade the English Courts either to set aside the judgment under the English CPR 3.9[2] or which will persuade the English Court of Appeal to reopen the matter pursuant to rule 52.17 of the English CPR, it would be unjust for the judgments to remain enforceable here while Mr Ablyazov continues to pursue a process which may result in the English judgments being set aside. I am prepared to assume in Mr Ablyazov's favour that he has a real prospect of persuading the ECtHR to recommend that the English judgments be set aside and that he has a similarly real prospect of persuading the English Courts in the light of such a ruling that they should be set aside. In those circumstances, Mr Hayman submits, it would not be 'just and convenient' within the meaning of section 3(1) of the Act to register the judgments here (or alternatively the right course would be to suspend their operation until the processes of the ECtHR are complete and their fall out ascertained) because there is a real risk that Mr Ablazov may suffer irreversible damage if the judgments are executed and the Bank is unable to comply with any order that might be made for restitution as an indirect consequence of a favourable ruling from the ECtHR. I am also prepared to assume in Mr Ablyazov's favour, but without deciding, that that risk is real.

---

[1] registration means that the judgments take effect as if made by the High Court here in the BVI
[2] which permits the Court to set aside a default judgment

[9]   I am not persuaded by these submissions. While the scheme of the Act is to give the High Court in the BVI a discretion whether or not to register judgments given in the High Courts of the United Kingdom, that discretion, given by subsection 3(1) of the Act, is subject to the other provisions of section 3. Thus, the BVI High Court may not register a judgment of the English High Court which is affected by any of the matters listed in subsections 3(2)(a) to (f). It is only if an English judgment is not so affected that the subsection 3(1) discretion arises. The discretion is to be exercised in favour of registration only where the BVI Court *'in all the circumstances of the case thinks that it is just and convenient that the judgment should be enforced in the Territory.'*

[10]   In ascertaining the meaning of these words where they occur in subsection 3(1) it must be borne in mind that any English judgment for which registration is sought will already have passed the subsection 3(2) tests, so that enforcement within the BVI will not offend any of the principles of private international law governing the enforcement of foreign judgments. Further, the English judgment debtor will have been afforded the additional protection, unavailable at common law, that the English judgment will not be enforced if it is, (or imminently will be) under appeal. At common law, there could be no defence to the enforcement of a foreign judgment satisfying these tests. In the light of this consideration, it seems to me that the discretionary words in subsection 3(1) are not to be construed as permitting the BVI Court to refuse registration on the grounds that it would be unjust for an English judgment satisfying subsection 3(2) to be enforced *at all*, but as conferring a discretion to refuse enforcement within the Territory under the Act if circumstances prevail which would render enforcement *within the Territory* unjust and/or inconvenient. That must be so, in my judgment, otherwise the local (BVI) Court would be in a position to refuse enforcement upon objections which had nothing to do with the Territory, but which amounted to challenges, direct or indirect, to the underlying justice of the processes which had culminated in the making of the English judgment.

[11]   I appreciate that as a matter of language Mr Hayman's alternative submission does not require me to pronounce upon the justice of the English processes which led up to the entry of the judgments. Instead, he says that it is the intended application to the ECtHR, coupled with the potential for the ultimate setting aside of the English judgments, that makes it unjust to enforce them now in the Territory. I do not regard that as a distinction of any significance. It remains the case that the submission that those circumstances make it unjust now to enforce the judgments in the BVI applies equally to enforcement in England, where no stay is in place and where enforcement is currently under way.[3] Mr Hayman is asking me to lean against enforcement on considerations of justice which are of universal application. If I were to decide, on the basis of Mr Hayman's submissions, that it would be unjust to enforce here I would necessarily be deciding that it would be

---

[3] Mr Ablyazov disputes that, because he says that the enforcement steps being taken are in fact being taken against the property of third parties, but I do not think that that matters for present purposes.

unjust to enforce anywhere, including in England. I do not believe that the Act is intended to confer upon the BVI Court in a case, such as the present, where subsection 3(2) is satisfied, a discretion to refuse registration and enforcement upon the grounds that a collateral challenge may cause the English judgment to be set aside. The scheme of the Act shows, in my judgment, that provided that subsection 3(2) is satisfied, the BVI Court must take the English judgment as it finds it. It is not entitled to speculate as to whether, in the long term, it will survive collateral attack.

[12]   I do not believe, therefore, that the discretionary words in subsection 3(1) of the Act are designed to permit the BVI Court to decide against enforcement upon grounds other than grounds peculiar to the Territory. For example, it would be both unjust and inconvenient to permit enforcement against a judgment debtor which had been put into insolvent liquidation in the Territory. Again, it would not be convenient to permit enforcement against a debtor with no assets in the Territory. Whatever may be the situations in which the BVI Court would be justified in refusing to permit enforcement of an English judgment in the Territory, it would seem to me to be extraordinary if the Court here could decline enforcement within the Territory of such a judgment on the grounds that at some indefinite time in the future it may cease to be enforceable in England for reasons not covered by subsection 3(2) and having no connection with the Territory.

[13]   On the contrary, if, contrary to my view, the BVI Court is entitled to take into account considerations of justice generally, I cannot see how it could be just to withhold enforcement within this jurisdiction of a judgment which satisfies subsection 3(2) and in respect of which no stay is in place in England, unless local considerations applied to make enforcement here either unjust or inconvenient. It is not suggested that there are any such.

[14]   So far as public policy is concerned, it seems to me that provided that subsection 3(2) is satisfied public policy requires that the provisions of the Act be given effect in this jurisdiction unless, which is not suggested, the causes of action relied upon in the English proceedings were such that the High Court here could not have entertained them on public policy grounds. It could not sensibly be suggested that that would have been the case. The Act was passed so that regular judgments of the English High Court could be enforced in this jurisdiction speedily and without complication. Once subsection 3(2)(f) is satisfied, as it is in this case, I consider that that is the relevant public policy to which this Court should have regard in deciding whether an English judgment should be registered and enforced here. It points in favour of enforcement.

Conclusion

[15]   This approach to the matter means that it is unnecessary for me to deal in any depth with the interesting submissions which were made as to the operation of the ECtHR and of

the Human Rights Act 1998. I intend no discourtesy to Counsel who have so skillfully advanced them by not dealing with those submissions as made, but I am satisfied, for the reasons which I have attempted to give above, that it is neither unjust nor inconvenient for these judgments to be enforced in this jurisdiction. On the contrary, it seems to me to be both just and convenient that they should be. For those reasons, this application fails.

[16]   I stress that nothing in this judgment should be taken as an indication of this Court's opinion as to the likelihood that Mr Ablyazov will succeed in having the judgments set aside through his intended applications to the ECtHR. I have no opinion about that one way or the other.

Commercial Court Judge
2 May 2013

22 0ct 2015 Hogan Lovells Secures Success in UK Supreme Court for BTA Bank in Ablyazov Fraud Case

News: Press Releases | 22 October 2015

Hogan Lovells Secures Success in UK Supreme Court for BTA Bank in Ablyazov Fraud Case

21 October 2015 · Hogan Lovells has achieved a further landmark judgment for BTA Bank in one of the biggest fraud cases to have ever come before the English courts. Today the Supreme Court has ruled in favour of BTA Bank in relation to its appeal over Mr Ablyazov's use of unusual loan arrangements to circumvent spending restrictions contained in the English standard form freezing order.

The judgment relates to four loan agreements with two BVI companies, worth £40 million in total, which Mr Ablyazov took out while his assets were frozen by the worldwide freezing order obtained by BTA Bank at the outset of the English proceedings. Mr Ablyazov directed the lenders to pay monies to fund his solicitors, the solicitors of other defendants and various other third parties, without disclosing details of those payments to BTA Bank or the court. The Supreme Court has today unanimously ruled that Mr Ablyazov's secret funding arrangements were in fact captured by the terms of the freezing order, and were therefore subject to the restrictions and disclosure obligations contained within it. In doing so, the Supreme Court has overturned the previous decisions at first instance and in the Court of Appeal.

This is the first time the Supreme Court has been asked to interpret the standard form freezing injunction and the ruling sets a precedent for future English freezing orders. The Hogan Lovells team advising BTA Bank was led by London litigation partners Chris Hardman and Alex Sciannaca, supported by associate Tom Devine.

Commenting on the judgment, Alex Sciannaca said:

"This is the first time that the Supreme Court has been called upon to rule on the Bank's continuing proceedings to recover the billions of dollars stolen from it by Mr Ablyazov.

"We welcome this decision, which confirms that the huge loan agreements that Mr

other undisclosed payments to third parties - were captured by the freezing order, meaning
that those payments should have been subject to the scrutiny of the Bank and the court all
along.

*"The Supreme Court's judgment closes a loophole in the freezing order regime that
unscrupulous defendants such as Mr Ablyazov have previously sought to exploit."*

ENDS

Notes to Editors

- BTA Bank launched global legal proceedings against Mukhtar Ablyazov and his associates in 2009 after auditors at PwC identified a massive hole – more than $10 billion – in the Bank's balance sheets. This led to the discovery of a large-scale fraud committed by Mukhtar Ablyazov while he was Chairman of the Bank.
- The legal proceedings in England consist of 11 claims filed by BTA Bank in the English High Court seeking to recover more than US$6 billion in assets misappropriated by Mr Ablyazov. The Bank has secured judgments for more than US$4.5 billion and is in the process of seeking to enforce those judgments against assets currently held in receivership.
- As previously reported, Mr Ablyazov was found guilty of contempt of court in February 2012 and sentenced to three concurrent 22 month prison sentences. Mr Ablyazov fled the jurisdiction before sentencing and was subsequently debarred from defending various claims brought against him by BTA Bank. His appeals against the contempt and debarral orders were dismissed by the Court of Appeal in November 2012, with Lord Justice Maurice Kay observing that "It is difficult to imagine a party to commercial litigation who has acted with more cynicism, opportunism and deviousness towards court orders than Mr. Ablyazov". On 26 February 2013, the Supreme Court of the United Kingdom refused Mr Ablyazov's application for permission to appeal the debarral judgment.
- Mr Ablyazov is currently in prison in France. In January 2014, The Court in Aix-en-Provence granted both the Russian and Ukrainian requests to extradite Mr Ablyazov. However, the decision was annulled by the French Court of Appeal in April because of a procedural error made by the court. The case was sent for re-trial in the Court of Lyon. In October 2014, The Court of Lyon granted both Russia and Ukraine's requests to extradite Mr Ablyazov. Mr Ablyazov once again appealed the decision. In March 2015, the French Supreme Court upheld the earlier ruling by the Court of Lyon to extradite Mukhtar Ablyazov to Russia or Ukraine. In October 2015, it was reported in the French media that the French Prime Minister has issued a decree for the extradition of Mr Ablyazov to Russia.
- Hogan Lovells has been acting for the Bank since May 2009 in its series of major fraud cases before the English Courts. The Bank was represented in this appeal by Hogan Lovells partners Chris Hardman and Alex Sciannaca, with support from associate Tom Devine.

Share Back To Listing

21 MARCH 2018 BTA Bank (Respondent) v Khrapunov (Appellant)

PRESS SUMMARY

21 March 2018

JSC BTA Bank (Respondent) v Khrapunov (Appellant) [2018] UKSC 19
On appeal from [2017] EWCA Civ 40

JUSTICES: Lord Mance (Deputy President), Lord Sumption, Lord Hodge, Lord Lloyd-Jones, Lord Briggs

BACKGROUND TO THE APPEAL

From 2005 to 2009 Mr Mukhtar Ablyazov was the chairman and controlling shareholder of the respondent, a bank incorporated in Kazakhstan. He was removed from office when the bank was nationalised in 2009. He fled to England where he obtained asylum. The bank brought various claims against him in the High Court. The bank alleged that he had embezzled some US$6 billion of its funds. At the outset of the litigation, the bank obtained an order requiring Mr Ablyazov to identify and disclose the whereabouts of his assets and a worldwide freezing order preventing him from dealing with them. In 2010 the High Court appointed receivers over his assets. It later transpired that Mr Ablyazov had failed to disclose large numbers of undisclosed assets, which he had sought to place beyond the reach of the claimants through a network of undisclosed companies. In 2011 the bank consequently obtained an order committing Mr Ablyazov for contempt of court. He was sentenced to 22 months' imprisonment. By the time the judgment had been handed down, however, Mr Ablyazov had fled the country. His whereabouts are unknown. Default judgments in the sum of US$4.6 billion have been obtained against him, but very little has been recovered.

In 2015 the bank brought the present claim against Mr Ablyazov and his son-in-law, Mr Khrapunov, who lives in Switzerland. The bank alleged that Mr Khrapunov, being aware of the freezing and receivership orders, entered into a "combination" or understanding with Mr Ablyazov to help dissipate and conceal his assets. The judge found that it was sufficiently established for the purposes of this application that they entered into it in England. Mr Khrapunov is said to have been instrumental in the dealings of assets held by foreign companies and in concealing what became of those assets. His actions are said to constitute the tort of conspiracy to cause financial loss to the bank by unlawful means, namely serial breaches of the freezing and receivership orders in contempt of court. This appeal concerns only the position of Mr Khrapunov, who unsuccessfully applied to contest the jurisdiction of the High Court. The Court of Appeal dismissed his appeal.

JUDGMENT

The Supreme Court unanimously dismisses the appeal. Lord Sumption and Lord Lloyd-Jones give the lead judgment, with which Lord Mance, Lord Hodge and Lord Briggs agree.

REASONS FOR THE JUDGMENT

Mr Khrapunov's first argument was that contempt of court cannot constitute the required "unlawful means" for the tort of conspiracy to cause loss by unlawful means, because contempt is not a wrong which by itself entitles a claimant to sue the contemnor: it is not "actionable". Therefore, he argued, there was no good, arguable case against him on which to found jurisdiction [5].

The tort of conspiracy can be divided into "lawful means" conspiracy and "unlawful means" conspiracy, although that terminology is inexact. A person has a right to advance his own interests by lawful means, even if the foreseeable consequence is damage to the interests of others. Where he seeks to do so by unlawful means, he has no such right. The same is true where the means are lawful but the predominant intention of the defendant is to injure the claimant, rather than to further some legitimate interest of his own. In either case, there is no just cause or excuse for the "combination" with others. Conspiracy being a tort of primary liability, rather than simply a form of joint liability, the question what constitutes unlawful means cannot depend on whether their use would give rise to a different cause of action independent of conspiracy. The correct test is whether there is a just cause or excuse for the defendants combining with each other to use unlawful means. That depends on (i) the nature of the unlawfulness; and (ii) its relationship with the resultant damage to the claimant [8-11].

Unlike various other legal duties, compliance with the criminal law is a universal obligation. The unlawful means relied on in this case are contempt of court, which is a criminal offence. For that purpose, the defendant must have intended to damage the bank. The damage to the bank need not have been the predominant purpose, but it must be more than incidental. The defendants' predominant purpose in this case was to further Mr Ablyazov's financial interests as they conceived them to be. But the damage to the bank was necessarily intended. Their aim was to prevent the bank from enforcing its claims against Mr Ablyazov, and both defendants must have appreciated that the benefit to him was exactly concomitant with the detriment to the bank. The damage was not just incidental [15-16].

It was argued on behalf of Mr Khrapunov that the existence of a claim for conspiracy to commit contempt of court would be inconsistent with public policy because it would substitute a remedy as of right for one which depended on the discretion of the court. The Court satisfied that there is no such public policy [18-23].

The matters alleged by the bank, if proved, would amount to the tort of conspiracy to injure by unlawful means [24].

Mr Khrapunov's second argument was that the English courts lacked jurisdiction by reason of the general rule, in article 2 of the Lugano Convention to which both the UK and Switzerland are parties, that a person should be sued in the Convention state in which he or she is domiciled. The sole currently relevant exception to that rule is article 5(3), which allows a claim in tort in the Convention state "where the harmful event occurred or may occur". Article 5(3) is substantially identical to article 5(3) of the Brussels Regulation (Council Regulation (EC) No 44/2001). The Court of Justice of the European Union ("CJEU") has interpreted the latter to cover both: (a) the place where the damage occurred and (b) the place of the event giving rise to it [26-28].

As an exception to the general rule, article 5(3) must be interpreted strictly. Although there is no basis for interpreting it by reference to national rules of non-contractual liability, those national rules are relevant. They define the legally relevant conduct and whether an event is harmful. The CJEU has repeatedly focused on the relevant harmful event which sets the tort in motion. This gives effect to an important policy of the Brussels/Lugano scheme by promoting a connecting factor with the jurisdiction of a court which is particularly close to the cause of the damage. In *Cartel Damage Claims (CDC) Hydrogen Peroxide SA v Akzo Nobel NV* (Case C-352/13) [2015] QB 906 the CJEU identified the formation of a cartel, not its implementation, as "the event giving rise to the damage" [31-40].

The Court of Appeal correctly identified the place where the conspiratorial agreement was made as the place of the event which gives rise to and is at the origin of the damage. In entering into the agreement, Mr Khrapunov would have encouraged and procured the commission of unlawful acts by agreeing to help Mr Ablyazov to carry the scheme into effect. Thereafter, Mr Khrapunov's alleged dealing with the assets the subject of the court order would have been undertaken pursuant to and in implementation of that agreement. The making of the agreement should be regarded as the harmful event which set the tort in motion [41].

References in square brackets are to paragraphs in the judgment
NOTE
This summary is provided to assist in understanding the Court's decision. It does not form part of the reasons for the decision. The full judgment of the Court is the only authoritative document. Judgments are public documents and are available at: http://supremecourt.uk/decided-cases/index.html

21 June 2018 Approval of judgement against Mukhtar Ablyazov and Ilyas Khrapunov

IN THE HIGH COURT OF JUSTICE
BUSINESS AND PROPERTY COURTS
OF ENGLAND AND WALES
COMMERCIAL COURT (QBD)
His Honour Judge Waksman QC sitting
as a Judge of the High Court

Claim No. CL-2015-000549

B E T W E E N:

JSC BTA BANK

Claimant / Applicant

-and-

MUKHTAR ABLYAZOV

First Defendant

ILYAS KHRAPUNOV

Second Defendant / Respondent

Thursday, 21 June 2018

Approved Judgment

HHJ WAKSMAN QC:

1. Today, 21 June 2018, was the date set for the cross-examination of Mr Ilyas Khrapunov, the second defendant to these proceedings which were commenced against him by the JSC BTA Bank (the "Bank") in 2015 along with the first defendant, Mr Ablyazov.

2. The underlying claim was that Mr Khrapunov had conspired with Mr Ablyazov to break the terms of an original freezing order and a receivership order granted against Mr Ablyazov by effecting or assisting the removal or transfer of a number of funds so as to take those funds out of the reach of the freezing order against Mr Ablyazov and thus to assist him in evading and breaking clear court orders.

3. One particular claim concerns what is called the A and N Project Monies; it is dealt with in the Amended Particulars of Claim at paragraphs 26(a) to 26(f). The allegation is that back in 2011, Mr Khrapunov engaged a corporate services provider, Mr Aggarwal, to administer assets for Mr Ablyazov.

4. Mr Aggarwal was an English accountant, but well versed in making use of offshore companies and other entities by which the true ownership of particular assets could be concealed. Mr Aggarwal provided services to Mr Khrapunov, and Mr Khrapunov told Mr Aggarwal he was acting on behalf of a number of clients, but did not reveal the truth, which was that his true client was in fact Mr Ablyazov. In late 2011, some $56 million was paid to companies administered by Mr Aggarwal on the instructions of Mr Khrapunov; then, between late December 2011 and October 2012, further sums totalling $439 million were paid to a different company, incorporated in the Seychelles but also administered by Mr Aggarwal, for no or no sufficient consideration. The effect of all of that was that Mr Aggarwal, acting on the instructions of Mr Khrapunov, effected the transfer of all of those monies, which in fact were at all material times the assets of Mr Ablyazov. The allegation is that Mr Khrapunov knew perfectly well what

he was doing which was to assist Mr Ablyazov to evade the court orders to which I have referred.

5. Unsurprisingly, the losses claimed, inter alia, against Mr Khrapunov in this respect consist of the monies which had been illicitly transferred in this way on the footing that, if those monies had not been transferred, they would be now available for execution in respect of the several very large judgments which have been awarded already against Mr Ablyazov. That is the underlying claim which is relevant for today's purposes.

6. A number of interim measures were granted by this court over a number of years against Mr Khrapunov in order to secure the claims against him. They included a worldwide freezing order made as long ago as July 2015, by Mr Justice Males. That order contained information requirements by which Mr Khrapunov was to provide not only details of his personal assets, but also details of his dealings with Mr Ablyazov's assets. Mr Khrapunov signally failed to deal with those disclosure requirements.

7. Subsequently, he was ordered to attend for cross-examination, originally by Mr Justice Teare, in March 2016. He appealed that decision, inter alia, on the basis that, if he were to come to England to be cross-examined, he was likely to be the subject of an extradition request by the Governments of Kazakhstan and Ukraine, which would expose him to all sorts of serious risks.

8. The Court of Appeal dealt with that appeal on 27 March of this year. At paragraphs 18 and 19, the court held that, having regard to the previous history of non-disclosure by Mr Khrapunov and other matters, the Bank had a good arguable case that he had lied in the disclosure he had given, in the same way that it had a good arguable case that he had lied in the disclosure he gave in relation to non-personal assets. The application for permission to appeal against the order for cross-examination was refused in May 2016 by Lord Justice Moore-Bick and was certified as totally without merit. That was in respect of cross-examination in principle.

9. There was a compelling case for the Bank to be able to cross-examine Mr Khrapunov.

10. What Mr Khrapunov then did was raise the question of extradition and the risk to him, before Mr Justice Phillips, as a reason why he should not come to England to be cross-examined, but, instead should be cross-examined by video-link from Switzerland. The learned judge rejected that application. He said that, on the basis that there was no extradition arrangement between the UK and Kazakhstan, and given the absence of any example of an ad hoc extradition arrangement, the risk of arrest with a view to extradition to Kazakhstan, if Mr Khrapunov came to England, was effectively non-existent, it was certainly no greater than any continued risk to Mr Khrapunov in Switzerland, where he was then based, and there was no risk of extradition to Russia or Ukraine either.

11. The Court of Appeal was equally unimpressed with the risk of extradition argument. If he was arrested here pursuant to a Red Notice, Ukraine, which was one of the other countries that he referred to, would be given an opportunity to put in evidence to say there was no impediment to extradition to Ukraine. Ukraine might be able to show it was now a safe place to which he could be extradited, but on the evidence, the Court of Appeal thought that possibility was speculative and the prospects of it being able to do so were low -- low but not completely unreal or fanciful. Then, as to the conditions under which he would be retained in the UK, the likelihood was that he would be granted conditional bail pending the decision on any extradition request, at most which would be six to nine months.

12. In dealing with the detriment that he would suffer if he came to the UK, the appellant said only that he found it distressing to be separated from his wife and children but it was not suggested there was any serious difficulty of them coming to England to live with him while he was on bail, nor was it suggested there was any other significant detriment.

13. Then, drawing all of those threads together, and having given detailed consideration to the

relevant law, and in particular the Polanski case, the Court of Appeal held:

"The order for cross-examination was granted in order to make the freezing order against him as effective as possible.... The administration of justice is liable to be brought into disrepute if the court is disabled from enforcing a freezing order in the most effective way. That would be the effect of granting a variation of the 23 March order proposed by [Mr Khrapunov], to substitute cross-examination in Switzerland for cross-examination in the High Court in London" (paragraph 91).

14. At paragraph 94, they said that they "consider that the Bank has made out a strong case that the appellant has been involved in assisting in a massive international fraud and is concealing evidence about relevant assets. The public interest in the court trying to give maximum practical effect to the freezing order ... is strong". It may be, the court opined in paragraph 97, that Mr Khrapunov would refuse to come to the High Court for cross-examination anyway, but the court would be perceived as bowing to blackmail by him and would be liable to bring the administration of justice here into disrepute if it simply accepted the assertion he would not come, with, as they put it, " a shrug of the shoulders and a sigh". Therefore, as they state in paragraph 99, they dismissed the appeal and ordered that there should be cross-examination on a confidential timetable.

15. That date is today. As effectively threatened or promised by Mr Khrapunov, he has not attended. That is the background.

16. His non-attendance today is of particular relevance because of an unless order made by Mr Justice Males on 25 May 2018. That followed an application on the basis that there had been numerous defaults by Mr Khrapunov in relation to the payments of costs orders and also a failure to attend on an initial occasion for cross-examination. All I need do is read the body of the order. At paragraph 2, it says this:

"Unless Mr Khrapunov fully and properly complies with each of the following orders by the following deadlines ..." – then they are set out – "... (i) those parts of his Amended Defence dated 31 October 2017 which address the Relevant Claims shall stand struck out and Mr Khrapunov shall be debarred from defending the proceedings insofar as they concern the Relevant Claims and (ii) the Bank shall be at liberty to enter judgment against Mr Khrapunov in relation to the Relevant Claims."

17. The particular matters which he now had to comply with were the payment of various costs orders and also having now to attend for cross-examination.

18. As is evidenced by his non-appearance today, which was the date set for cross-examination, as he well knew, there is a breach of every part of the unless order, and the Bank has applied for there to be judgment in default. This occasion was used to deal with that application as well, and this was also identified to Mr Khrapunov.

19. On the face of the order and the non-compliance, the defence to the Relevant Claims (as defined in the unless order), which is that part that I recited, is struck out and the Bank is entitled to judgment in default.

20. Before dealing further with the nature of the particular order sought, I should recite that, yet again, Mr Khrapunov has said that he cannot, and will not, come into this jurisdiction for any purpose because of the risk of extradition. He said that both in respect of the video-link for his cross-examination, but also because he said that an hour would not be enough for this application for judgment in default. I do not know on what basis he says that, since it is an entirely simple application and, indeed, in other circumstances, it might have been dealt with by way of an administrative request.

21. But what effectively he does is to say again that there is a risk of extradition, this time adding that if that happened, he was then at risk of torture or even death. But, in essence, he is putting forward the same sort of reasons as he had put forward before Mr Justice Phillips and which

were rejected by both him and the Court of Appeal.

22. It also is in keeping with the last time when he invoked such reasons, which was to deal with an application that he was going to make to the Commercial Court, which concerned his application to set aside some parts of an order -- the order of Mr Justice Teare made back on 23 March 2016. All of this came before Mr Justice Popplewell on 18 May of this year but part of what Mr Khrapunov wanted then was to adjourn his own application, partly he said because he can't afford a lawyer and, secondly, again, because of the risk of extradition to the Ukraine and Kazakhstan.

23. I am not going to read the text of Mr Justice Popplewell's judgment. It is not necessary for me to do so, save that in paragraph 21 through to paragraph 27, the learned judge, in a comprehensive and careful fashion, explained why it was that the extradition arguments in particular had no merit whatsoever. I come to the same conclusion today.

24. Therefore, there is no reason why I should not deal with the application for default judgment today. The truth of the matter is that Mr Khrapunov has the means and the ability to come here, if he wished, to object to this judgment in default or indeed to put submissions in writing as to why it should not be made, since this is an interlocutory matter and where no oral evidence will be taken. But he has not done anything of that kind. There is, therefore, no obstacle at all to my making the judgment in default as requested by the claimant.

25. So far as the detail is concerned, the amount, as I have indicated, is the specific amount claimed by way of damages in the Amended Particulars of Claim. It constitutes a claim for a specific amount of money.

26. The only reason why this was not done by administrative request is because the unless order only operates in respect of part of the claim against Mr Khrapunov, and where, in those circumstances, a party seeks judgment in default of only part of a claim, it is obliged to make an

application on notice, which is what has happened here.

27. The total principal sum claimed is $495.8 million. The Bank has discounted that to avoid any risk of double recovery, which concerns some New York proceedings, and the Bank has agreed to limit the sum claimed to US$424,110,000. The last transfer of the A and N Project Monies was 1 January 2014, and the Bank is content for interest to start then and not any earlier.

28. Although higher figures have been awarded, particularly by this court, including in related litigation concerning Mr Ablyazov, the Bank here seeks simply 4 per cent as a flat rate of interest for all of the relevant period. That seems to me to be eminently reasonable and appropriate.

29. Therefore, the interest claimed, at least to 5 July, would be a further US$76 million-odd. It seems to me that that needs to be adjusted so that the appropriate figure to today's date can be given as pre-judgment interest.

30. I agree with the suggestion in paragraph 19.6 of the Bank's skeleton argument that the rate for post-judgment interest should be less than the 8 per cent prescribed by the Judgments Act, which is really quite out of keeping today with current levels of interest, and, therefore, I will substitute the rate of 5 per cent going forwards.

oOo

High Court: 'no merit' to Kazakh's extradition fears in £4.6bn fraud hearing

By Max Walters | 29 August 2018

The High Court has said there is 'no merit whatsoever' in claims by a Kazakhstani man accused over his part in a $6bn (£4.6bn) alleged fraud alongside his former banking executive father-in-law that returning to the UK for questioning would put him at risk of extradition.

In a ruling published this week, His Honour Judge David Waksman said there was no risk that Ilyas Khrapunov would be extradited from his current base in Switzerland to either Kazakhstan or Russia.

Waksman granted a default judgment in favour of BTA, finding Khrapunov liable for conspiring with Mukhtar Ablyazov. Khrapunov has been ordered to pay more than $424m (£229m), plus $75m interest.

Khrapunov is the son-in-law of the former chief executive of BTA Bank Ablyazov. He is accused of conspiring with Ablyazov to remove funds out of the reach of a previously granted freezing order.

According to Hogan Lovells, which represented BTA Bank, the case is one of the biggest fraud cases to have ever come before the English courts.

Khrapunov had previously been asked to attend court for questioning but declined citing extradition fears. Addressing those fears, Waksman wrote: 'The truth of the matter is Khrapunov has the means and the ability to come here, if he wished, to object to this judgment...but he has not done anything of that kind. There is, therefore, no obstacle at all to my making the judgment in default as requested by the claimant.'

Richard Lewis, partner at Hogan Lovells, said: 'This is an important decision, a key step forward in BTA's attempts to recover the huge sums that have been misappropriated from it and the culmination of three years of intense litigation against Khrapunov, including important decisions in the Court of Appeal and Supreme Court that are likely to make it easier for fraud claimants to obtain redress in the English courts in the future.'

In March, the UK Supreme Court ruled that the English courts had jurisdiction to hear BTA's claims. It dismissed Khrapunov's claims that, as he is domiciled in Switzerland, the English courts had no jurisdiction over him.

However, the court cited the Lugano Convention, to which both the UK and Switzerland are parties, and which allows a claim to be pursued in the jurisdiction 'where the harmful event occurred or may occur'. As the agreement between Khrapunov and Ablyazov was entered into in England, even though the breaches took place elsewhere, the court said the English courts could have jurisdiction.

The legal proceedings in England consist of 11 claims filed by BTA Bank in the High Court seeking to recover the funds misappropriated by Ablyazov. The bank has previously secured judgments for more than US$4.5 billion and is in the process of seeking to enforce those judgments.

Acting for BTA Bank Hogan Lovells instructed Stephen Smith QC and Tim Akkouh of Erskine Chambers. Hughmans Solicitors, which instructed Littleton Chambers' Charles Samek QC and Mark Delehanty acted for Khrapunov.

Ministry
of Foreign Affairs
Republic of Poland

Faithful to my Homeland, the Republic of Poland

NEWS   MINISTRY · FOREIGN POLICY · TRAVEL TO POLAND   SEARCH   Q

NEWS

- PRESS OFFICE
- POLISH DIGITAL DIPLOMACY
- PHOTOS & VIDEO
- SPEECHES OF THE MINISTER

PHOTOS & VIDEO

POLISH DIGITAL DIPLOMACY

SPEECHES OF THE MINISTER

The MSZ asked The Open Dialog Foundation to promptly send all of its resolutions adopted in 2013-2017 and to provide a number of explanations.

In a letter addressed to the President of the Management Board of The Open Dialog Foundation, Lyudmyla Kozlovska, the Ministry of Foreign Affairs – in performance of its oversight obligation towards the foundation – asked for all of the foundation's management board's resolutions adopted since 2013 until today to be promptly handed over.

In addition, the MFA asked for a clarification why the foundation's official Facebook profile includes calls for illegal actions, such as encouraging people not to pay taxes. The ministry also asked for an explanation why the foundation's representatives publish content in social media which are personal attacks on specific persons.

MFA Press Office

PRINT

SHARE:

SHARE

0

SEE MORE

INDEX